Also by Mary Moody and published by Murdoch Books

Au Revoir (2007)
Mary Moody's Roses (2006)

Last Tango in Toulouse

MARY MOODY

Last Tango
in Toulouse

Torn between two loves

PIER 9

First published in 2003 by Pan Macmillan Australia Pty Ltd.
This edition published in 2007 by Pier 9,
an imprint of Murdoch Books Pty Limited
www.murdochbooks.com.au

Murdoch Books UK Limited
Erico House, 6th Floor
93–99 Upper Richmond Road
Putney, London SW15 2TG
Phone: +44 (0) 20 8785 5995
Fax: +44 (0) 20 8785 5985

Murdoch Books Australia
Pier 8/9
23 Hickson Road
Millers Point NSW 2000
Phone: +61 (0)2 8220 2000
Fax: +61 (0)2 8220 2558

Chief Executive: Juliet Rogers
Publishing Director: Kay Scarlett

Typeset in New Baskerville by Midland Typesetters
Cover and text design by Ellie Exarchos
Cover photograph by Getty Images

Printed by 1010 Printing International Limited in 2007.
PRINTED IN CHINA.

A catalogue record for this book is available from the British Library.
ISBN 978 1 92125 947 0
ISBN 1 92125 947 7

This book is dedicated to my husband, David, who, in spite of his pain, gave me ceaseless love and support throughout the roller-coaster ride of the last few years.

There was a little girl
Who had a little curl
Right in the middle of her forehead
When she was good she was very, very good
And when she was bad she was horrid
Henry Wadsworth Longfellow

ACKNOWLEDGEMENTS

I would like to thank my children, Tony, Miriam, Aaron and Ethan, and their partners, Simone, Rick, Lorna and Lynne, for always supporting me, even if they didn't agree at times with what I was doing. And for allowing themselves to be a part of the story, however painful.

I would like to thank my two dearest friends – Christine Whiston in Australia and Jan Barwick-Claudy in France – for lending a sympathetic ear and never judging me.

Also our neighbours in Yetholme, Sue and Robert Porter, who were always there for David when I was in France and he was at the farm alone. And Kaye Healey who supported us both, again without judgement.

Last but not least I am indebted to my editor Debra Adelaide for her generous contribution to both *Au Revoir* and *Last Tango in Toulouse*.

1

If running away from home for six months to live in an ancient village in rural France is the fantasy of every middle-aged woman, then I feel as though I have been living the dream for all of them. The year I turned fifty I set off alone on a sabbatical to escape from my demanding career and large family and live in southwest France. It was a watershed year in my life. There were many reasons why I felt driven on that particular journey, but I realise now that I was only vaguely aware of them at the time. I certainly didn't expect that my time alone would have repercussions that would change my life in so many ways. Nor did I realise that I was entering a critical and confusing phase when all aspects of my past life would come under scrutiny, from my work and family priorities to my most intimate personal relationships. Perhaps if I had known in advance I would never have dared embark on this risky mid-life adventure, because some of the changes have been painful and the pain has been felt deeply – not just by me, but by my entire family.

When I experienced the overwhelming urge to run away I was entering the early stages of that female demon, the menopause – the roller-coaster ride of years which some women glide through without batting an eyelid and others rage through in a sweaty battle of hormones, rocketing emotions and inner angst. I fall into the latter category.

The fact that I found mid-life so difficult to negotiate was a great surprise to my husband and children, and even more of a shock to me. As a younger woman I sailed relatively unscathed through my pregnancies and births and always revelled in motherhood. Later I embraced becoming a grandmother with delight. I had, with seemingly little effort, juggled a fairly high-powered career, an ever-expanding family, a high-maintenance garden, a three-decade relationship with my husband David and even the trials and tribulations of a live-in mother who, for the most part, was more of a joy than a burden.

So why now, when the future is so rosy and the world around me secure after many years of financial struggle, am I suddenly so unsettled and restless? Has running away from all my responsibilities for six months uncovered a wellspring of hidden unhappiness that is causing all the certainties of my life to unravel before my eyes? And is there, therefore, an inherent risk in selfishly following my dreams? Would it be better to just shrug my shoulders and accept life as it is without ever taking any risks? I don't think so.

While I was in France I wrote a book about my physical and emotional journey. *Au Revoir* gave me an opportunity to reflect on the ups and downs of my life and to chart my reasons for needing to escape. In the process of writing this book I quickly discovered that there was a vast difference between talking about life's sad or difficult moments and actually committing them to paper. By documenting events from my sometimes painful childhood, I believe I finally confronted their impact for the first time.

Being alone in France also gave me a chance to think deeply about my relationship with my husband David. It forced me not only to examine our past but to contemplate our future together. With our children grown and out of the nest, everything now depended on just the two of us, and I was not entirely convinced that I wanted to spend the rest of my life with him, even though I knew I still cared for him deeply. Complicating matters was an unexpected surge of sexuality which at the time caused havoc all around me. I met a man and fell in love and found myself having to negotiate that most difficult of all balancing acts – trying to keep my marriage and family intact while having an affair.

During this turbulent period there were many other changes in our lives. We bought a small village house in a little-known region in the southwest of France, known as the Lot, because of my desire to re-experience the joys of my new-found freedom; we left our much loved house and garden in the Blue Mountains and moved to a farm in the small rural hamlet of Yetholme near Bathurst; I abandoned my career on television and took a new direction that saw me travelling overseas for at least half of every year. And I went on a search for my long-lost sister Margaret, to finally piece together the jigsaw of my early life. It was at times an intensely painful journey, but it brought with it moments of great joy and self-discovery.

For most of us, living safely within the confines of our familiar comfort zone is much easier and certainly less confronting than plunging headlong into the unknown. The older we get, the more difficult it is to take risks and establish new patterns of behaviour, to make new friends or experiment with living in a foreign culture or to consider abandoning an entire way of life. While we change externally, as nature takes its toll on our faces and bodies, inside we are at risk of becoming more cautious and more conservative.

From what has been written about my age group – the baby boomers – I understand that there is a common desire to fight the natural aging process on every level. Although, as a young woman, the notion that growing older could be a problem never occurred to me, when I hit fifty I suddenly started to resent the possibility that my life could become less exciting. Instead of growing old gracefully, I yearned to break out of the mould, to escape from my responsibilities and obligations; I also wanted to remain youthful and vibrant, both physically and mentally. I wanted new challenges and new excitement and even, perhaps, new dangers. I wanted to be outrageous and experiment with a few things I hadn't tried before, to break a few taboos.

This desire to live every moment of life to the full is no doubt deeply connected to the hormonal changes that most women experience in mid-life. It must be very disturbing for those who have delayed having babies until their late thirties to confront this urgent restlessness when they still have school lunches to pack and Saturday morning sports to attend. At least I was in the fortunate position, with my children fully grown and completely independent, to be able to indulge myself in the desire for freedom that was overwhelming me.

During the blissfully irresponsible period I spent in France, I enjoyed, for the first time ever, a breathing space that allowed me time to think about and reflect upon my life to date. It was quite cathartic looking back to my childhood and the difficulties of my family life with parents who were brilliantly clever but deeply flawed – alcoholic, left-wing political rebels who tried to live within the 1950s ultra-conservative social culture. It was also humbling to look back at my years as a parent and to realise that, despite the best of intentions, I had also made so many blunders, in many ways not dissimilar to those made by my own parents. Most painfully, it was illuminating to look back on my marriage, which I had always regarded as solid as a rock and admit that in my heart there were many areas of difficulty and frustration. No different, I have no doubt, from many long-term relationships, yet confronting for me now to consider so deeply.

During this period of reflection I also started to look ahead to what I wanted for the remainder of my life, for the next twenty or thirty years. Should I go on as I had always done, clinging to the stability of my large, extended family of children and in-laws and grandchildren, which had always seemed at the heart of my very existence? Or should I make radical changes that could have disastrous consequences for my family life?

2

Returning home after my liberating time in France, I immediately threw myself back into the all-too-familiar pressures of work and family life. I had urgent deadlines for magazine articles and botanical photographs to supply to publishers and, with Christmas imminent, I was faced with a mad scramble of preparations – the pine tree to decorate, food shopping for the eighteen or so people who would participate in our usual celebratory lunch and, of course, last-minute presents and treats to buy for grandchildren.

Still jet-lagged, and also keenly culture-lagged after such a long time immersed in rural French life, I raced around getting organised and trying desperately to fit back into my 'real' life. I experienced a few hair-raising moments readjusting to driving on the left-hand side of the road, the same problems in reverse as when I first learnt to drive in France the previous June. After being away so long I realised I was looking at my old, familiar surroundings with a fresh eye, an eye that had adjusted to the simplicity of small French villages and open green fields.

Although we tend to believe that Australia is relatively under-populated, I found coming home exactly the opposite. Where I had been living in France was so tranquil and uncluttered compared with the upper Blue Mountains where we had been living and working for twenty-five years. The school holiday throng of tourists, the lack of parking and the general down-at-heel appearance of so many streetscapes grated on my new-found sensibilities.

The day before Christmas I had what I can only describe as an epiphany on Katoomba Street. Caught up in yet another irri-tating traffic jam on this steeply sloping stretch of road that leads tourists to the famous Three Sisters Lookout, I was overcome with an intense feeling of frustration. I simply didn't relate to this place any more. I didn't like it and I didn't want to be here. I don't know exactly *where* I wanted to be, but it wasn't in Katoomba or even in our pretty village of Leura, which had changed so drastically in character over the last decade.

When we first moved to the Blue Mountains in the late 1970s, Leura was a quiet backwater. There was one small teashop in the main street and many of the other shops were either vacant or stocked with half-empty shelves. On Sunday morning you could have easily fired a cannon down the main street of Leura Mall without the risk of hitting anybody. Then the mountains enjoyed a tourism renaissance, becoming as they had been in the 1920s and 1930s, a popular weekend and holiday destination. Guest-houses and B&Bs started hanging out welcome signs all over the Upper Mountains, and more than half the shops in the main street were converted into trendy cafes or bistros. While the influx of tourists did wonders for the prosperity of local business life and therefore the economy, there had been a definite downside for local residents. Over the past few years parking in the village had become impossible, even after an entire back-block of houses was cleared to create an extensive new car parking area. Up to a dozen huge tour buses would park in a side street every day, disgorging hundreds of sightseers wanting to cruise the shops or stop for a coffee. As a result, shopping locally became very expensive, with most retail outlets charging tourist prices, forcing residents to travel further afield to the supermarkets instead of patronising the local corner store (which, in turn, was eventually converted into yet another stylish cafe!). Certainly the village centre looked charming because of the money spent on tarting up shop facades and maintaining the pretty gardens that line the footpath and the central strip. But it was no longer possible to stop quickly to pick up a loaf of bread or a newspaper without double parking and causing traffic chaos, then running the gauntlet of the crowds walking four deep down the footpath.

The day before Christmas I announced to my amazed husband that I wanted to sell up and move out. He had only just recovered from the shock of my desire to buy a house in a foreign country and now it seemed I was hell-bent on dragging him away from a house and garden that he adored, nestled in a community where he felt absolutely at home.

Generally men are less thrilled at the prospect of change than women. David, in particular, is a man who hates even the slightest disruption to his set pattern of life. The simple act of rearranging the living room furniture can send him into a steep decline, so my new idea of abandoning the house in which we had reared our children and the garden that I had slaved in (not to mention spent a fortune on) for more than two decades brought him totally undone. He was convinced that I had lost the plot, and put up strong objections to my idea.

'I thought we would stay here forever,' he lamented. 'I was planning to die here.'

With a wry but determined smile I told him it could 'possibly be arranged'.

He began to realise that I was deadly serious.

The essence of my argument for selling up and moving was the dawning realisation that our way of life in the mountains had been destroyed by development and tourism, and that we needed to look for a quieter place – perhaps even the farm that I had always dreamt about.

For me the final straw was the ugly and invasive red trolley tour bus. Phoney San Francisco-style dark red buses take tourists on whistlestop tours to all the main beauty spots and attractions in Leura and Katoomba. For almost a year I had been aware of them buzzing down our street eight times a day, but what I didn't realise was that our house and garden was actually part of the tour. How many mornings did I wander out in my slippers to deposit the recycling bin on the footpath only to be confronted by a bus loaded with wide-eyed tourists gazing in our direction? A friend, recently moved to the district, decided to take the tour out of interest, and immediately phoned me to report in malicious delight.

'They come down your street and the guide tells them, "Look to your right and see the house and garden of the television lifestyle presenter and garden writer, Mary Moody",' he said.

The irony is that most of the tourists are foreign, generally Asian, and obviously wouldn't have the vaguest idea about local television programs or personalities. While I laughed heartily at the notion of being part of the local equivalent of those tacky Hollywood celebrity tours, I also felt a strong sense of being invaded. It sharpened my resolve that leaving our home in the mountains was the only option open to us.

3

Meanwhile, I urgently needed to turn my mind to the task of finishing *Au Revoir*, the book I had started writing about my adventures the previous year in France.

One of the basic guidelines drummed into me as a young reporter back in the 1960s was that 'good journalists' never put themselves forward, never project their own personality or viewpoint into the interview or article. I had spent most of my journalistic career either interviewing newsworthy people or researching factual topics for magazine articles or television segments, so finding myself suddenly writing about my own life was quite a challenge. During the last twenty-five years working as an editor or author of gardening books I have, from time to time, injected a little of my own philosophy and personality into the business of being a gardener. Yet I have tended to maintain those old-fashioned journalistic rules about being an observer rather than a participant. Besides, writing columns and books aimed at helping people grow better cabbages hardly allows the writer to include a lot of personal information.

However, *Au Revoir* demanded something quite different of me, and I had to completely rethink the boundaries of the writing style I had adhered to for so many decades. My first thought was that I should write a sort of middle-aged woman's travelogue/adventure story with lots of detail about the local food and customs in rural France. It didn't turn out that way.

Initially, while gallivanting around the French countryside, eating and drinking myself into oblivion, I didn't even consider putting pen to paper. After all, sitting down to write every day for hours in order to meet a deadline was exactly the sort of pressure I was escaping from. I had a loose agreement with the publishers that I might or might not describe my personal and physical progress during this odyssey, but under no circumstances was I going to allow it to cramp my style. After several months of self-indulgence I finally realised that I could, without feeling too constrained, document some of my impressions of the region of France to which I had made my escape.

At the forefront of my mind was the conversation I had had back in Sydney with my agent and my publisher before I left home, discussing the style of the book and the voice that would relate the story. They both felt it was not enough simply to start at the beginning of the actual journey to France, where I set off in search of some personal space and freedom. They believed that I needed to elaborate on some aspects of my earlier life that would help to explain why I felt so compelled to take time out. They were convinced that I had to paint a fuller picture in order to justify my sudden flight from home, family and responsibility. But the thought of describing the personal details of my life felt totally bizarre. I didn't know where to start and was convinced, quite cynically, that nobody would be all that interested anyway.

Most journalists have an inbuilt suspicion of 'autobiography' – weighty books written by those who happen to be in public life and believe themselves to be significant enough in the scheme of things to set out the fine detail of their lives for all to appreciate and admire; or by sporting heroes who, apart from scoring a few triumphant goals, haven't even really lived a life. The thought of this style of book sent a shiver of revulsion down my spine and almost caused me not to start writing at all.

My next obstacle was deciding which voice to write in. It is very difficult to write in the first person when you have been trained to avoid using the words 'I' and 'me' in your work. Feeling a sense of panic and a total lack of confidence in setting down even the first sentence, I phoned my agent at her Sydney office.

'Who is supposed to be telling this story?' I asked. 'What is the tense – past, present or future? I don't know where to begin.'

She advised me to start at the beginning: to write about my childhood and take it from there.

'It's your own story, so it's just a matter of telling it from the heart,' she added.

Early in the morning the next day, when my brain was relatively fresh I sat down to write. I gathered my memories together and started to recall what it was like being the child of alcoholic journalist parents who were also communists, living in what would now be described as a 'dysfunctional family' complete with domestic violence, infidelity and suicide. I wrote about it exactly as I remembered it, the good bits and the bad bits. The fact was that my home was often an exciting and stimulating household filled with the witty banter of authors and artists, but it also frequently deteriorated into a terrifying environment for a small child, with drunken brawling, bailiffs banging on the door because of unpaid bills and neighbours reporting 'disturbances' to the police.

I wrote about my two sisters – Margaret, who fled from the family on her eighteenth birthday and never looked back, and Jane, who died at the age of eleven months under circumstances I have never really understood. And about my two brothers – Jon, who seemed to survive relatively unscathed and went to sea in his teens, and Daniel, fourteen months my senior, who also left home to make his way in the world as soon as he possibly could.

For the first time, in writing down these memories, I tackled them head on as I had never done before. I sat at the computer in that tiny room in a medieval French village as the words tumbled out, with hot tears of anguish rolling down my cheeks. It wasn't so much self-pity – although I did feel a lot of pain for that little girl all those years ago, coping with the hardships of her young life – but a cathartic realisation that I had never really come to terms with it all. That while I had always openly discussed incidents remembered from childhood, even joked about them with my family and friends at various times over the years, I had never fully confronted the fear and pain I had experienced all those decades ago.

Writing it down didn't necessarily give me a deeper understanding of what had gone on between my parents, but it helped me clarify my own feelings about what it was like being a member of my family – of being the only girl who remained after Margaret and Jane had both vanished from my life, and how my two brothers had emerged in their different ways from the same unhappy environment. It all came out very quickly, like a flood, as thoughts and words cascaded onto the keyboard, but I thought it would all probably be edited out at the end of the day. After all, who would be interested in the ravings of a middle-aged woman about her troubled childhood?

Despite my anguish, I didn't write in a bleak or tortured manner. Instead I tried to be upbeat, even vaguely bemused, about the circumstances of my childhood. More or less, I suppose, the way I believed I coped with it during my adult life.

Next I wrote about my eccentric mother Muriel, who lived with David and me and our four children for nearly twenty-five years. Having a permanent extended family is unusual today, so I wrote quite honestly and with some humour about the ups and downs of my strong relationship with her and then about her sudden death. Muriel had a profound and very positive effect on our children's lives, and it was quite poignant remembering some of the funny and sad things that happened during our long time together. Eventually the story reached the point where I set out for France and writing the next part – my French adventure story – was great fun. I delivered a semi-completed manuscript to my agent and my publisher a few weeks after I returned home.

Their reaction was as I expected: the book needed a good rewrite and a strong edit. What I hadn't expected was that they both felt it needed more, much more, about the personal side of my life. The editor thought so too. She combed through the manuscript, making copious notes about the areas she thought should be fleshed out: more on my relationships with my mother and my daughter; more on my marriage; more on my feelings about myself – my body image, my sexuality, my thoughts and the reactions to the people I met while living overseas.

By now I was beginning to have doubts about the wisdom of exposing my private life in such a candid fashion. The prospect of pouring even more of my soul onto paper was daunting but, being so deadline-oriented (a result of years of journalistic paranoia), I put my head down and wrote like a madwoman. I started to wonder who I was actually writing this book for: for myself (a little); for the readers (I had my doubts); for the publishers (most urgently).

I wondered if I was just reconfirming that lifelong role I had created for myself of doing what others expected of me rather than what I wanted to do for myself. Despite my reservations, I handed the finished manuscript in on time and then immediately tried to forget about it and get on with the other parts of my life – my family, my work on the gardening program and the plan I had for moving us from Leura to somewhere quieter and more rural.

Buying a piece of property in a foreign country is a major commitment, especially in a place as far removed from Australia as southwest France. While David and I still wondered, from time to time, if our decision to buy a rundown piece of real estate in France had been rash, we were committed to the idea of spending at least part of every northern hemisphere summer in our small village of Frayssinet-le-Gelat. The house itself was typical of thousands of deserted dwellings in France that are up for grabs by anyone willing to take them on. Every rural area has vacant properties that come on and off the real estate market according to the whim of the owner or, more precisely, the multiple owners, because this is one of the main factors influencing the abandonment of so many village and country houses. According to the French inheritance laws, which date back to Napoleonic times, no descendant – legitimate or illegitimate – can be excluded from an inheritance. This means that when a property owner dies there is frequently a brawl among the members of the family about what to do with it. Properties often sit vacant for decades, crumbling with neglect, because no decision can be made that will satisfy all the parties involved.

When I was dashing around the countryside looking at vacant properties, I saw several attractive but derelict houses that had been vacant for thirty or forty years, or even longer. One in particular that I loved hadn't been occupied since 1932. But David and I made a more conservative choice – a small village house in need of some renovation but still quite livable.

In rural France, when abandoned properties eventually become available for sale, they are sometimes bought by the commune (council) to renovate for a specific community project. When we took our first steps towards buying the little house in Frayssinet-le-Gelat, we had to wait until the house was offered first to the mairie, the governing body of the council, because they always have first right of refusal. This is more of a formality than a sticking point; seldom will the mairie vote against a house being sold. They are generally quite relieved to see houses being occupied, even if only by part-time foreign residents, rather than remaining empty and falling into further disrepair. If the mairie did for some reason wish to acquire a property that was in the process of being sold privately it could cause all sorts of problems that could only be resolved in the law courts. Fortunately, in our case, the local Mayor had no objection to our proposed purchase. He even rushed the paperwork through for us because we had to sign all the legal documentation before we returned to Australia.

Local government is very powerful in France and the local mairie (the name of both the town hall itself and the local council) is the centre of virtually all legal bureaucracy; it is certainly where all the important decisions that affect the commune are made. The size of the Conseil Municipal depends on the number of people in the commune. In Frayssinet-le-Gelat we have thirteen representatives, very similar to our local government councillors here in Australia, although the election method is slightly different. Prospective candidates put their names forward and this list is posted prior to election day. In small communes of less than 3500, names can be added to the list regardless of whether their owners have asked to be nominated – in other words, people in the community who are well liked might find themselves elected to office, like it or not! These elected representatives, who will govern for seven years, then vote for the Mairie (or Mayor) from among their number, and he or she has tremendous powers. The Mairie administers the local budget (drawn from the rates), performs marriage ceremonies and signs death and birth certificates; he or she also acts as police sheriff of the commune, in charge of security, and has the final say on all matters of law in the commune. The councillors, also known as advisers, are given specific areas to administer – it could be road maintenance or the organisation of local festivities such as village feasts or celebrations. Local government lies at the heart of the commune and everyone is passionately interested in local political matters.

There are several English families already living either full- or part-time in the village and now, of course, a couple of Australians who will come and go and create a ripple of local interest. The post office opens only three mornings a week and there are rumours that it might close due to lack of business, not unlike post offices in country towns all over Australia. The rumours spur the locals into writing letters and sending cards and packages once again, in fear of losing this wonderful traditional service. There is a local school that takes children through infants and primary; then they must travel to Prayssac or Cahors for secondary education. There are two bars, one of which also operates as a pizzeria restaurant; there's a very fine charcuterie run by the local butcher who is a highly respected figure in the community and always prepares the main course for the village feasts in the surrounding region; and there's an alimentation, or corner store, which stocks all the convenience items any local resident or holiday-maker could require, from light bulbs to gourmet cheeses to regional wines and boot polish. The boulangerie is also very well regarded in the district, and locals have their cakes and tarts for birthday and anniversary celebrations made to order rather than going to the bother of making them themselves. There is also a garage that sells bottled gas for cooking stoves as well as petrol, and you can register your car and have all manner of mechanical and electrical repairs done there. Indeed, if you didn't feel the need to see a doctor or dentist you could cheerfully stay put in Frayssinet-le-Gelat twenty-four hours a day every day of the year. It is a self-contained haven, and many of the older locals rarely step outside the village precinct; it's much easier to shop locally than go through the hassle of driving to a larger centre further afield in search of a supermarket or hardware store.

Several decades ago the village would have contained a much wider range of shops and services. The church would have been open for mass every Sunday instead of just one Sunday in four. There would have been a village doctor and midwife and other shops, such as the hairdresser's which once occupied the front part of our downstairs main room. The fact that locals can now drive to a larger centre, perhaps only ten kilometres away, has meant that these facilities have become more spread out among the villages.

Exploring the village backstreets and byways, I am enchanted by the number of gardens, especially potagers, that are tucked away in every corner. I sometimes wonder how the weekly markets make a profit when so many people grow their own produce, but I am quite relieved when I realise that my own little house and courtyard has no space for such an endeavour – the only two plants are an old red climbing rose and a wisteria which have tangled together to create a mass of colour every spring over the old stone barn. I am perfectly happy to leave it at that! This may surprise friends who regard me as a committed gardener but I am well aware of how impossible it is to maintain a garden when you are around for only a few months each year. Other part-time foreign residents in the village pay a small fortune for their gardens to be tended in their absence, and I know that we will have expenses enough with the house without having to pay for the garden.

My lack of passion for gardening in France also reminds me that I have changed quite a bit over the last few years. Once I would visualise garden beds and pots overflowing with flowers at every opportunity, but now I feel quite ambivalent about all the work involved. It seems to me that I have spent half my adult life on my hands and knees weeding. Now I am wanting to move on to other things.

My film-making husband David is a passionate man who can be exasperating to live with because of his entrenched attitudes towards all aspects of life. He's not a flexible or easygoing person in any sense, and we have clashed frequently over all sorts of trivial, day-to-day incidents and concerns. He is inclined to get upset about things that most people regard as unimportant, and he is a man with a strong sense of routine and order, baulking at spontaneity or unexpected change. He likes things the way they are because it makes him feel secure.

That said, he is also a highly charged creative individual, very loving and loyal to his family and friends and seldom boring to be around. He is a Scot by ancestry, and many of the character traits attributed to that race apply to him. He's careful and considered, pedantic and exacting, and in many ways quite conservative, despite his appearance and the fact that over the years he has been responsible for producing or working on films that could be considered radical. He is therefore a contradiction in many respects. On the one hand, when working with script-writers and film directors and actors he can be inspirational with his intense enthusiasm and deep commitment to the project. At the same time he can be dour and negative, tending to anticipate the worst in any situation. When he is in this frame of mind or when he plummets, as he sometimes does, into a deep depression, I wonder what on earth I am doing with him.

My ancestry is more on the Irish side, and I have the opposite disposition to my husband. I never worry myself about trivial matters, am irresponsible with money, laugh at situations that others would find grim, and generally regard most days as an opportunity for a celebration or a party. Yet somehow, despite our opposing personalities, we have weathered more than three decades of mostly happy cohabitation.

One of the main reasons our relationship has survived is because, over the years, we have spent quite a lot of time apart. David's career took him to Sydney every week, where he stayed three or four nights, sleeping in the back room of his office, being available for phone calls and meetings with his working colleagues twenty-four hours a day. He also spent long periods away from home filming or doing research for various film projects – in the United States, England, Ireland, Scotland, South Africa, Turkey, France and Asia. His career has given him great satisfaction and provided financial security for our family, but I always felt it was at the expense of his involvement and participation as a husband and father. He enjoyed considerable success with many of his films, producing more than forty features that have been screened in cinemas and on television all over the world. In the late 1980s he made a controversial anti-apartheid film, *Mapantsula*, which was widely screened, received awards at several major film festivals and eventually earned him the 1988 Human Rights Australia Film Award.

I was so proud of his achievements and his commitment to a risky cause, but my pride was tinged with bitterness. That particular film took David away from us for nine months, and when he returned he found living in Australia and being with his family an anticlimax after the intensity and danger of the film-making experience. He and his fellow film-makers had smuggled the film out of the country under the nose of South African Security so that it could be completed in London in time for the Cannes Film Festival (where it was an official selection). David felt such a buzz of excitement at their success that I suppose it was natural he would find home life boring by comparison. For me, this rankled.

I also experienced a certain level of tension when David was at home, and I realise now, many years later, that it was because of our situation, having my mother Muriel under the same roof. While having Mum around was fantastic for me while David was absent, when he was at home it could be fraught with difficulties. Neither my mother nor I was prepared to hand over the reins to David when he walked in the door. We were accustomed to working together as a team, running the house and the garden and rearing the children. If David had strong opinions about how we were managing, especially in relation to the children, it could result in an instant explosion – usually from Muriel rather than me. At times they got along together brilliantly, especially in the last few years of her life. However, there were often long periods when the situation was pretty grim and I took on the role of peacekeeper, trying to calm down the situation however I could.

In many respects my relationship with David was muffled by the constant presence of another adult in the house. I felt that I had given David permission to be an absent husband and father by not fighting against it more forcefully, not insisting that he spend more time at home and get more involved in the children's lives. But I can now see that life was easier without him around. There was less conflict. And when he was around the last thing I wanted was to engage him in a fight about how I was feeling. If I had tackled him verbally for what I considered to be his shortcomings, Muriel would undoubtedly have jumped on the bandwagon and life would have been totally unbearable.

So I put up and shut up. For almost twenty-five years I danced a jig around my husband and my mother so that the family would remain on an even keel. Mum was by no means an easy person to live with either. Opinionated, forceful and quick-tempered, she required a good deal of careful handling, and again it was up to me to keep her mood buoyant. Most of the time we had an excellent relationship – very open, very honest and very affectionate. We agreed on so many things, from politics to cooking, and I loved her dearly although I also found her exasperating. So there I was, stuck between two lovable but demanding people, with four growing and boisterous children to bolster the equation.

A couple of times – perhaps three times – during this period I decided that I couldn't stand it any more, that I should leave David and start a new life somewhere else. I am sure every marriage has moments like this. But there was really no possibility of it ever happening. If I left David, would I also leave my mother? Or would I leave them alone together and just take the children? A ridiculous notion. Even though I was working,

I couldn't afford to support my mother as well as four children and I was loath to break up the family. So I stayed put and made the best of it. To all intents and purposes we were one big happy family and, mostly, we were, but a lot of this fell on my shoulders. I took responsibility not just for the physical and emotional well-being of my family, but for the entire mood of the household. If you ask any of my adult children now, they will say they had a totally happy and carefree childhood, and for that I feel satisfaction.

David's justification for being distracted from the family, when things did occasionally come to a head, was always that it was the nature of his business that required his absence. That he was doing it for all of us. That he didn't enjoy being away for such long periods, indeed he often felt depressed and despondent when away from home so much. That he had no choice. That he was not trained or qualified in any other area and could find no alternative employment. He was trapped in his working life and that's just the way it had to be.

My counter argument would always be that even when he was at home he didn't 'engage' with the family. He complained of being exhausted by the intensity of his working life and would frequently spend long hours when at home stretched out on the sofa reading the weekend papers cover to cover, recovering for his return to Sydney the following Monday. However, during the weekends he readily made himself available for his work colleagues, who would phone any time of the day or night, often needing his counselling or support with a film project. Scriptwriters – such a needy lot – were the worst. One in partic-ular had uncanny timing, phoning on Sunday just as I was setting out the family lunch. David should have been the one to carve the roast, but often this was left to me because he would take the call and speak for an hour, sometimes longer, propping up the writer's fragile ego while his lunch congealed on the plate. This used to drive me crazy. I was the one dashing to Saturday morning sports and doing the shopping and mowing the lawn, although he did eventually take on some of these chores. I dealt with my dissatisfaction by drinking lots of beer and cooking up large, happy family meals that brought cheer to the household. I kept it all together, but underneath there was a simmering of discontent and resentment, seldom acknowledged but ever present.

The other vital aspect to this whole relationship equation was love. When I wasn't furious with David or frustrated by his intransigence or enraged by his stubbornness, I was in love with him. Our personal relationship was loving and passionate and this always undid me in the end. Just when I thought I could walk away from our marriage he would make contact with me on such an intimate level that the thought of leaving him was impossible. We were bound together by something that was difficult to explain, that was more than just our mutual adoration of our children or the physical joy of our sex life. Something intangible kept us together and helped us survive. I always knew that he loved me deeply and this constancy gave our union security.

But now, in middle age, I have started to question seriously whether love is enough. Whether all those years of sublimating my feelings for the sake of family harmony can be wiped away by love. Should I be grateful that I have a man who loves me? After all, many people don't have love in their lives and would regard me as reckless for throwing away a husband who adores me and whom I certainly love in return. For reasons I can't really explain, however, I am no longer prepared to live in a situation that doesn't work for me. I am no longer prepared to compromise. It's a major dilemma, one that I am going to have to confront once and for all.

The first people to live in our little village house in
France were our son Ethan, then just 21, and his girlfriend Lynne, who was about the same age. As soon as
we arrived back in Australia and announced we had found a
place they started saving to make the trip. Within five months
they had arrived in Frayssinet with little or no French language
skills and only meagre savings.

Our friends in France welcomed them with open arms,
nicknamed them 'the kids' and even provided some local work
for Ethan using his horticultural qualifications. The plan was
that they would do some basic renovations, such as chipping off
crepi (mortar) and painting, in return for the house, rent-free.
They intended to stay for six or twelve months, depending on
how their finances lasted, but this idea was quickly squashed
when Lynne found herself unexpectedly pregnant.

What was meant to be a carefree working holiday turned into
a bit of a nightmare for Lynne. She was desperately morning sick
and homesick and missing the support of her mother and sisters

during such a difficult time. Neither Ethan nor Lynne had planned to have a child at this stage of their relationship and, while they were excited, they were also daunted and I think a little frightened at the prospect of parenthood. Both of them came from largish families, both of them adored babies and children, but it meant that their time in France was to be foreshortened; and for Lynne it meant a lot of time alone – and feeling frightful into the bargain. Ethan was frequently working during the week and the constant aromas of rich French food cooking in the village added to her nausea. She made a lot of friends who were supportive, and when Ethan was working she did some tentative exploring, but the very nature of her pregnancy limited her ability to enjoy the experience of living in a foreign country.

The weekends were easier for them both – Ethan was at home and they could do things together, even if it was only starting some of the preliminary renovations. One Saturday he decided to clean out the upper level of the barn, which was piled high with all sorts of junk and mounds of dirt – it's quite a mystery why anyone would shovel dirt up to a first floor. The window at that level had no glass, so Ethan simply shovelled the rubbish into the courtyard below, intending to take it by trailer to the tip at a later stage. The first thing he discovered in the gloom, after erecting a portable light to work by, were dozens of beautiful old timber trugs – purpose-made agricultural baskets for carrying produce such as walnuts, chestnuts or apples. Some of the trugs had a mesh base for allowing dirt to pass through; they must have been made for harvesting potatoes and other root crops. He dusted them off and put them out in the sunshine for closer inspection. Some were badly eaten by woodworm, but many were quite perfect, with beautiful bent willow handles. On closer inspection he also found a whole range of tools and templates for making trugs, including a vice-like piece of equipment that was obviously used for forming the arched handles from water-soaked willow stems. He realised that the barn, in a previous incarnation, had been a workshop for making these agricultural baskets, all of which were stamped on the side with the word LEROUX.

Later, he noticed a framed black and white photograph on the kitchen wall of our friend and neighbour, Danny. It was of the village in the early twentieth century. There was our house, with the name LEROUX out the front and the downstairs shutters opened to the street, making a shop entrance. It seems that part of the main downstairs room was a shop selling these gardening artefacts; this was quite a coincidence given that Ethan and I are both such keen gardeners and have strong horticultural connections in our work. It made him believe the house had a special significance for us, that it was just right, meant to be.

Continuing the filthy and back-breaking task of shovelling barrowloads of dirt and other rubbish from the barn, he came across a folded length of old hessian buried deep within the debris. Pulling the light closer so that he could see better, he started to unravel the cloth, then reeled back in horror at the sight of a mummified dog corpse, obviously very ancient and somehow preserved in the dry soil where it had been interred probably close to a hundred years before. Why anyone would bury a dog on the upper level of a barn is beyond comprehension, unless it was a much loved hunting dog they couldn't bear to part with. Or perhaps it had died in midwinter and the ground had been too solid to dig a grave. It might have been stored in the barn awaiting later burial, then somehow forgotten. Ethan wasn't thrilled with the discovery and quickly repaired to the bar across the road for a few cleansing ales to recover from his experience.

For one of the months that Ethan and Lynne were in France I was leading a trek high in the Indian Himalayas. While travelling I bought a house-warming present for the French cottage – a colourful dhurry rug which was packaged up in the traditional hand-stitched calico wrapping and posted to Frayssinet. Instead of being delivered to the local post office as I expected, it was held in customs in Toulouse, which meant that Ethan and Lynne had to make the tedious journey to pick it up, not to mention paying a huge whack of import duty, which I had also not anticipated. Cheerfully they set out to find the customs depot, never easy given the peculiarities of French signposting and roundabouts. However, Ethan had become quite a skilled navigator of the road system and they managed to find the right place and pick up the parcel without too many problems.

On the return trip they were stopped by an official police roadblock, a not unusual occurrence at the entrances and exits of the motorways. Dozens of police and their intimidating-looking vehicles were parked to one side of the road and motorists were being flagged down randomly so that their papers and licences could be checked. Foreigners are required to always carry their passports as well as all the relevant papers for any vehicle they're driving; fortunately, Ethan was well prepared and all his documentation was quickly found to be in order. But when the police noticed the suspicious-looking fabric-wrapped parcel, postmarked from India, on the back seat a more serious and thorough search was made. 'The kids' were ordered from the car and Lynne's handbag was searched. Ethan was frisked, the boot was opened and they even checked under the seats, in the glove box and side compartments. The rubber floor mats were lifted. Ethan was given a sharp knife and ordered to unwrap the parcel on the side of the road, with several heavily armed police with machine guns over their shoulders standing over him. Shaking slightly, he cut through the needlework binding with the knife and unfolded the rug, spreading it out on the grass verge. The police crouched down, examining it closely, fingering the fringes and turning it over several times. Eventually they called their colleagues to come and look. Standing in a circle around the rug, they praised its design and colour, slapping Ethan on the back and telling him it was a 'très joli petit tapis' (a very pretty rug).

He quickly scooped it up, threw it onto the back seat and took off for the village and safety. He phoned me at home in Australia that night to berate me for setting him up with a suspicious-looking package from a Third World country.

Ethan and Lynne decided to stay in France until the sixth month of her pregnancy. They made the most of their time, travelling to Holland and then on to Paris by train and finally driving across the Pyrenees to Spain then down to the Mediterranean. It wasn't quite the carefree working holiday they had bargained for, but it was an exciting time as they came to terms with approaching parenthood and had their first taste of overseas travel. It could be a long time before they have such a chance again.

7

My desire to leave Leura and find a more tranquil rural lifestyle had not diminished, but David was still very anxious at the prospect of moving. We were now living alone and the location suited him perfectly – just an hour and a half from Sydney via the expressway, so he could go to Sydney for meetings and return the same day rather than staying away all week. He had changed his work routine and was no longer an absent husband. The irony of this was not lost on me. Our lives had become much less demanding with our children no longer living at home, and all the pressures of an extended family had vanished since the death of my mother. I sometimes wondered if Muriel's presence in the house had been one of the reasons for his lengthy absences over the years, but David assured me this wasn't so. It was pressure of work, simple as that, and he was pleased that I had my mother around for company and support while he was away, even if it had meant a weekend juggling act. Now he was virtually at home full-time and I wasn't sure I was thrilled with that option either.

Around this time our daughter Miriam, heavily pregnant with her fourth child, began to look for a larger house west of the Blue Mountains. She and her husband Rick searched initially in the Lithgow area, then eventually started looking in and around Bathurst, a country town we have always loved. Within weeks they put their house in Katoomba on the market and settled on a 1940s brick house in one of the more established streets of Bathurst. I was sad that the three little boys would now be more than an hour and a half from where we lived, as I had always enjoyed having them close by, but I fully appreciated their need to relocate. In many ways their reasons for wanting to leave the mountains, where Miriam had grown up, were the same as ours. They believed that the increase in population and the sheer number of tourists made the region not necessarily the best place to live, especially with young children. The streets had become very busy, the schools and local hospital overcrowded and Miriam, like me, had an idealised view of a suitable environment for children. The mountains had been perfect for my young family in the 1970s but were no longer perfect for her young family at the beginning of the new century.

Visiting them in Bathurst at the weekends, David and I started looking casually in the windows of real estate agencies and discovered that we could probably afford a small farm for what we could make selling our house and garden at Leura. To get a feeling of what was available in the district, we began looking more seriously at small properties. Almost immediately we found one that was absolutely perfect, within twenty-five minutes of Bathurst. It had everything we wanted. Only twenty-five acres – not too difficult to manage; a handsome old house in good condition with lots of open fireplaces and even a walk-in pantry;

pretty views all around and, best of all, unlimited water from a deep spring as well as a meandering stream and one good-sized dam. We were among the first people to be shown over this farm and as we walked around it became obvious to all three of us – Miriam had also come along for a look – that this was exactly right. David kept shooting me stern glances, trying to dampen my obvious enthusiasm in front of the real estate agent, but Miriam and I could barely contain our excitement.

In so many ways, this little farm epitomised the dream of rural life I had had when we moved to the mountains all those years ago.

In some ways, Leura had always been a compromise for me because I had wanted a proper farm, not just a house with a large garden. However, in those days (as now) farms closer to Sydney were way beyond our budget and farms further west were too far for David to commute. During all those years I had endeavoured to recreate a mini farm at Leura, and here at last was a real farm just ready for the taking. The prospect of my grandchildren exploring the paddocks and bushy areas around the farm filled me with happiness. Although we knew it would be financially very difficult in the short term because we were not ready to sell our Leura property, we decided to grab the opportunity because we realised that such an ideal place may not become available again. There were tenants in residence and we asked them to stay on until we were ready to move.

My gardening friends often ask me if it was heart-wrenching to leave behind a garden that took twenty years to create and I can only respond by saying that, in truth, it was easy. It was like the weight of the world being lifted from my shoulders. Somehow, my garden had become the symbol of my entrapment;

instead of being a joy and a release from the pressures of my working life, the garden had become just one more pressure in itself. It was all connected to my striving to maintain an image of perfection, of always being in control. And gardens, as nature rightly intended, are very difficult to control unless you spend hours a week tending them, or employ a small army of gardeners. I had endeavoured to create a low-maintenance garden but, by its very nature, the Leura garden required a huge amount of my attention and energy. It had a large area for growing vegetables and herbs; there were fruiting trees, bushes and vines, old and new roses, woodlands, perennial borders and an area for growing rare alpines. Not to mention dozens and dozens of potted plants that needed regular watering, feeding and fussing over. While I was overseas the weeds in the garden had really taken off. The beds were choked with buttercups and blackberry had seeded right through the shrubbed areas. Despite my attempts at mulching, the weeds were overwhelming and I was faced with weeks of back-breaking work to whip it into some sort of order so that I could continue using it as a location for filming the gardening program.

When I returned from France, I discovered that my heart wasn't in it. I could barely summon up the energy to spend two hours in the garden; the pleasure of it had gone. I hadn't lost interest in gardens or, more specifically, in plants. But the passion had dissipated. I still have no idea where it went.

My passion for my job as a presenter on the television program *Gardening Australia* had also severely waned, and it was only with effort that I maintained the enthusiasm to continue filming. Although I enjoyed strong relationships with the team – the researchers, producers and film crews in particular – I felt stale and jaded. I was also a little peeved at some of the attitudes of the ABC. The program had gradually become 'commercialised', with a whole range of gardening products being developed to be sold under the *Gardening Australia* banner in what is known inside the organisation as the 'Bananas in Pyjamas' factor. These days programs are expected to generate merchandise to turn a profit for ABC Enterprises, and I felt that this commercialisation was somehow undermining the independent integrity of the show. We had always prided ourselves on avoiding endorsements of products. Now, suddenly, we were being encouraged to promote our own range of gardening paraphernalia, exploiting the brand loyalty of our viewers. I believe the role of the ABC is to make fantastic television programs, not flog bags of potting mix, so this disenchantment added to my restless feelings.

In my typical fashion of handling pressure with humour, I decided to play a trick on the *Gardening Australia* magazine editors during a period when I was feeling particularly frustrated. I wrote a monthly column called 'Future Directions' which looked at scientific breakthroughs, in Australia and overseas, related to botany and horticulture. One month I put in a bogus item of news – created off the top of my head – just to see if anyone in the editorial department would notice. I made it pretty obvious that it was a joke and I intended to phone them after a week or so and point it out just in case it had slipped through the system.

Fragrant Solution

Disposal of dog manure has always been a huge problem for the French and now a group of their own local scientists has come up with a revolutionary and environmentally friendly solution. Using a heat treatment and a freeze-drying process they are converting the scooped-up poop into a rustic soap that is recommended for gardeners and outdoor workers. Marketed as 'Parfum de Merde', the soap comes in three colours and fragrances and is cleverly made into the shape of a small poodle. Cute!

The problem was that I wrote the item, giggled at my own naughtiness and promptly forgot all about it – until two months later, when I opened the latest edition of the magazine and there it was, in print. Nobody had thought it was a hoax and it had simply gone through the system without question. It made me realise that as presenters or gardening writers, we could say just about anything and people would believe us. When the 'powers that be' finally found out they were furious, but most of my workmates thought it was hilarious.

Once the decision had been made to move, and with the knowledge that I was soon to be released from all that hard work and commitment, I somehow managed to regain a little pleasure from my garden. I spent some relaxing days getting it ready to put the house on the market, freeing the beds of tangled weeds and turning over the soil which had become deep and rich during the twenty-five years I had cared for it. I looked fondly at the trees I had planted all those years ago, now well established and perfect in this setting. I pruned the roses, mulched the soil surface and even planted some vegetables for the summer months, knowing that I wouldn't be there to enjoy them. I felt no temptation to dig up plants and take them with me – not even the rare treasures I had painstakingly collected over the years.

A new life on the farm would liberate me from my twenty-five-year obsession with gardening and I was more than happy to let go of all the plants, in spite of the pleasure they had once brought me.

Occasionally I wondered if I was losing the plot a little, under-going such a radical change of heart. But it was all part of the new direction I was heading in – the future – which wouldn't involve an 'obligation' to keep up the image of the perfect wife, mother, gardener, writer, lover, cook and friend. There were many moments when I found it hard to believe it was really me making all these changes. It was as though a different woman had stepped into my shoes and was walking onwards, taking the real me along for the ride. The prospect of change was exciting, but it was also at times quite terrifying.

8

During my six months in France I desperately missed my grandchildren – much more than I missed my husband or even our own four adult children. Our daughter Miriam has three boisterous sons aged between seven and two and she enrolled at university to do a postgraduate degree. Her plans were suddenly thwarted when she discovered she was pregnant with a fourth child. These days large families are the exception, especially with parents as young as Miriam and her husband, Rick – both in their late twenties and already very much tied down with family responsibilities. Miriam was shocked and rather dismayed when she first realised she was carrying another child, but she quickly adjusted to the idea because she had so enjoyed her pregnancies and subsequent homebirths with Eamonn, Sam and Theo. I was still in France when she phoned me in tears, lamenting her career being put on hold for another child. However, within days she phoned back, laughing and excited at the prospect of another baby, and we discussed the possibility that perhaps, this time, she may have a daughter. In our family we have been very lucky with our mother–daughter relationships. I had a strong bond with my mother Muriel, who died suddenly after a lifetime as a heavy drinker and smoker, and I also enjoy an open and loving relationship with Miriam. I secretly hoped she would produce a girl so that she too could experience the joys of this female to female rapport.

Miriam and her entire family moved to Bathurst only eight weeks before the baby was due and she found the process stressful. Babies tend to be larger with each subsequent pregnancy; this baby was huge and pressing heavily down inside her pelvis. Packing up an entire house and juggling the needs of three other children took its toll. By the time the removalist truck had left she looked and felt exhausted. Unlike her earlier pregnancies, in which she had felt highly energised and powerful, this time she felt rundown and lethargic, so I spent a lot of time dashing back and forth between Leura and Bathurst, cooking meals and helping with the mountains of washing. When the birth was imminent I moved in with the family, sleeping on the sofa bed in the rumpus room. The three boys were well primed and prepared for the new arrival and this time – a first – Miriam had booked into the local hospital, just one block down the road.

There were various reasons for this decision, the first and most important being that there didn't appear to be a trained homebirth midwife operating in the district. The escalating cost of insurance has had a profound effect on independent midwives all over Australia, making it almost impossible for them to afford to practise – a similar situation to the one facing obstetricians in the private medical system, especially in rural areas.

Miriam and Rick were also rather strapped for cash, having just moved into a larger house and living on a single income with three hungry boys to feed. Homebirths are not covered by many private medical funds or even by Medicare, so those who opt for a home delivery must scrape together several thousand dollars to cover the midwifery fees. Lastly, Miriam had decided that, as she was so exhausted, a quick trip to hospital and back would be less work than having a home delivery. There's a great deal of mess to consider when you squat down and have a baby in the front room – groundsheets and dropsheets and water baths and medical equipment. It takes precision planning and organisation by the family, their support system and the midwife, and Miriam wasn't feeling up to it. She just wanted to pop this baby out then come home to a clean, quiet house with her darling family all around.

Usually, Miriam goes into labour about a week ahead of the due date, but this time she went full term and then nearly two weeks overdue. Each day the baby seemed to grow larger, making it difficult for her to walk, let alone bath and feed the other children or do any housework. Thank heavens I was around to help on the home front. As the days drifted by we discussed possible reasons for the late arrival – and finally I ventured to suggest that perhaps this baby didn't want to be born in hospital. There are so many factors involved in the onset of spontaneous labour and even to this day the medical profession doesn't really understand what triggers those first few genuine contractions. Miriam was having plenty of strong tightening sensations but established labour simply didn't want to kick in. In desperation we began to search for a midwife who might be persuaded to do a homebirth – I even offered to cover the fee should it be required.

After several hours on the phone we discovered a community midwife who once did homebirths in the district but was eventually squeezed out because of the insurance situation. She kindly came to visit and agreed that she would be prepared to deliver the baby at home, but there was one small hitch – all her delivery equipment was locked inside the community medical clinic and she wouldn't be able to retrieve it until Monday morning. It was Saturday, and the clinic closed for the weekend. We decided that if nothing happened before Monday, we would proceed with the homebirth plan. Miriam suddenly seemed so much more relaxed and happy and we began making practical preparations for a home delivery – baking bundles of sheets and towels in the oven, wrapped in brown paper, and preparing a sterile pack of tiny clothes for the newborn; exactly the same preparations we had made together three times before. Even though Miriam and Rick had felt quite comfortable with the idea of going to hospital, they were now thrilled at the prospect of changing their plans at the last minute and having the baby at home.

On Saturday night we fell into bed early, reasonably exhausted. Miriam hadn't been sleeping well because of the size of the infant. She couldn't get comfortable, and needed to get up and walk around from time to time when her back ached or erratic contractions woke her. I was woken at dawn by three small boys clambering over my bed and the family's overexcited Jack Russell terrier bouncing on my head. We tried to pass the Sunday as quietly as possible, with Miriam alternating between resting and walking. Rick took the boys to the park for a few hours and I continued with the mammoth task of keeping ahead of the washing. I wondered how it would be when there was also a new

baby to wash clothes for, and cloth nappies rather than dispos-
able. It was a totally daunting prospect.

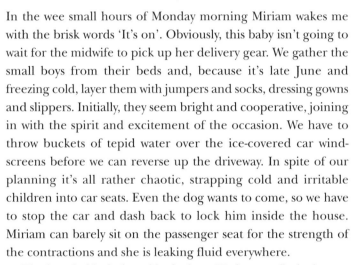

In the wee small hours of Monday morning Miriam wakes me
with the brisk words 'It's on'. Obviously, this baby isn't going to
wait for the midwife to pick up her delivery gear. We gather the
small boys from their beds and, because it's late June and
freezing cold, layer them with jumpers and socks, dressing gowns
and slippers. Initially, they seem bright and cooperative, joining
in with the spirit and excitement of the occasion. We have to
throw buckets of tepid water over the ice-covered car wind-
screens before we can reverse up the driveway. In spite of our
planning it's all rather chaotic, strapping cold and irritable
children into car seats. Even the dog wants to come, so we have
to stop the car and dash back to lock him inside the house.
Miriam can barely sit on the passenger seat for the strength of
the contractions and she is leaking fluid everywhere.

The hospital is dark and locked up. We have to find a buzzer
to alert the nurses in the casualty department. En masse we troop
along dark lonely corridors to the delivery rooms. There is a
woman in the last stages of labour in the first room we pass,
groaning and panting and reminding us how intense childbirth
is. The delivery rooms are plain but adequate, even though the
building is very old. There's a large comfortable room with a bed
and several lounge chairs, and a bathroom with a deep,
welcoming bath. Miriam wastes no time in jumping into the hot
water with Rick massaging her back. With her last two births she
spent most of the labour in a large portable watertub provided

by the midwife – it was big enough for Rick to get in and support her – although she always hopped out at the last moment when it was time to push. This bath is a conventional size, but Miriam finds the hot water comforting. We have phoned Miriam's close friend, Sandra, who is coming to help, and also my son Aaron's wife, Lorna. Miriam helped when Lorna was giving birth to their daughter Ella six months previously, and the two women have developed a close bond.

I also phone David in Leura so he can come quickly to Bathurst and take the small boys home. Unlike homebirth, where siblings wander in and out of the birthing room, having them in the hospital delivery room doesn't feel right. They quickly become bored and restless, and I am torn between trying to keep them amused and supporting Miriam in her labour. After the boys have been whisked away by their grandfather the atmosphere in the room becomes more relaxed and convivial. We share jokes between contractions and apply hot towels to Miriam's belly and back when the pains restart. We're a well-organised little team of five, so the hospital midwives leave us to get on with the job, doing just routine checking of foetal heart-beats as required.

Not long after daybreak Miriam starts to make the guttural sound in her throat that tells me she is ready to start pushing. I have been with her every step of the way through all of her births, a role that I treasure as a mother and grandmother. When her first son was born at their little house in Canberra, the midwife encouraged me to 'catch the baby' as it emerged, so that I could hand this precious new life to his mother. It was one of the most important moments of my life and my joy at each impending birth hasn't diminished.

Now I gaze from the hospital window at the new day. The rooms are on the second floor and the view to the surrounding countryside and hills is breathtaking. Even more so because of the sparkling white frost that has blanketed the entire landscape. I motion to Miriam, between contractions, suggesting that she have a quick look at this magical day that is about to herald the arrival of a new soul into the world. She groans impatiently at my suggestion, feeling far too weighed down to walk to the window. At that moment she is overwhelmed by her first pushing contraction, so I dash out the door and inform the midwife who has just come on duty that we are about to have a birth.

What follows is organised chaos. A bell rings and the doctor on call is summoned even though we know he won't be required to do much except watch. The midwife who will crown the head makes up a soft mat for herself so she can kneel on the ground – not the conventional hospital delivery mode but always Miriam's preferred position, on her knees with her head buried in Rick's lap. Sandra and Lorna continue to apply the hot towels to her back, and I take up a position to photograph the baby being born. Each birth has been well recorded and this one will be no exception. Just as the head – and a very large head it seems to be – is emerging the doctor rushes in, smiling and looking a little flustered. He's barely made it, and in coming into the room has blocked the natural light from the window that will make all the difference to my photographs.

'Would you mind moving over there?' I say rather cheekily. 'You're standing in my light.'

He agrees cheerfully and seems impressed by our well-oiled teamwork. Within moments the head and then the plump pink body of the baby emerges. The midwife passes it between

Miriam's legs, and she sits down cradling and kissing the child, who is now yelling mightily. Nobody speaks, allowing Miriam and Rick to discover the baby's sex at their own pace. She looks between the legs.

'Hello, Gus,' she says, sobbing and laughing simultaneously. 'Hello, little Gus, we love you.'

It's another boy and they have already chosen a name – Augustus James, after my mother's father from Wales. Gus for short. Gus isn't so little. He's a mighty 4.3 kilos and perfect in every way.

Miriam catches my eye.

'Do you realise what day it is?' she asks.

'Monday?' I venture.

'No, the date. It's the 25th. Your birthday. You and Gus have the same birthday.'

I am overjoyed at this realisation – he's the best birthday present I have ever had.

Within an hour Miriam is up and about, moving to a ward because the delivery room is suddenly required for another woman in labour. I go back to the house and rescue David, who has been struggling to entertain three overexcited and by now overtired small boys. I get them dressed ready for school and kindy, and together we take them back to the hospital to meet their new little brother. At first they seem slightly overawed, but nevertheless impressed. I take them to their various day activities and then go back to the house to ready it for Miriam, Rick and Gus to come home. I put a heater in the bedroom and make up the bed with fresh sheets. I start a pot of chicken soup and set the open fire. By lunchtime they are home safe and sound and Miriam snuggles into bed with her now sleeping infant. It's such a beautiful scene, and one that never fails to move me, those first few precious hours shared with this new life.

We all agree that Gus was never meant to be a girl. He's just perfect being Gus – my birthday boy.

9

 The changes that were happening in all our lives became more apparent soon after the birth of little Gus. I finally made a complete break from my ABC job and then David and I shifted from our Leura house and garden to the farm near Bathurst. Although he was still unsettled by the pace of change, David was steadfastly supportive and even attempted to be cheerful about the farm and the countless irritating problems associated with the move. Statistically, a large percentage of Australians sell up and move house every four or five years, but for us the relocation was traumatic because we had lived in the same house for twenty-five years. The volume of possessions accumulated over a third of a lifetime is mind-boggling and I found myself spending many long days in the attic and garage, sorting through the detritus of our life. David has been a hoarder all his life, both in his office and in his personal life. He has accumulated the most alarming collection of film and sound tapes, trade magazines, film and TV scripts, correspondence, old cheque books and even clothes that no longer fit him or have been inherited from deceased relatives. His most bizarre collection is of second-hand golf balls discovered lying abandoned in 'the rough' during a two-year period when he was seriously engaged in a daily walking exercise regime around the local golf course. He painstakingly collected more than 600 balls, sorting them into batches of sixty in recycled plastic bread bags which in turn have been gathered into recycled plastic shopping bags in batches of five.

Over the years we have had blazing rows about these sorts of things. I think he should just give the bloody golf balls to someone who actually plays golf but he can't bring himself to part with the wretched things. He also has dozens of those little sponge bags that airlines give away with fluffy socks and toothpaste. He can't throw these out either. In my previous life I would simply shrug and allow these irritating obsessions to wash over me, but in my recent more restless frame of mind I have became increasingly impatient with my husband's odd and irritating habits. Most of the time, though, I didn't have the energy to fight, let alone win, these battles, and because there seemed so little time to get organised for the big move, we threw everything into boxes, bags and crates and then into the boot of the car and dragged it all out to the farm. Golf balls included.

We moved our animals, including cats, dog, chickens and ducks. We stacked the contents of both our working offices into one of the large farm sheds because we had nothing set up in the house by way of computer tables or bookshelves or working surfaces. That would have to come later. Having moved most of the small bits and pieces ourselves, we eventually hired a removal company to take all the furniture across. It was a mammoth task, taking more than twelve hours, even though the farm is little more than an hour from Leura. We both vowed this would be the last time we ever moved.

During times of stress – and moving house is always a very stressful time – conflict can arise, even for couples who don't normally exchange cross words. Part of the reason that David and I have moved house only twice in our entire time together is that it's the obvious catalyst for tension. This time we seemed to be at loggerheads for days, even weeks. Once again my current mood dictated my inability to tolerate the frustration of his obsessiveness about every fine detail. I have a very pragmatic – he would say offhand – attitude towards material possessions: if they are lost or broken they can always be replaced. David, on the other hand, worries about every last item, and to me it seems such a waste of time trying to keep track of so many trivial bits and pieces.

David has always had a tendency to put on weight, even back in his early thirties when we were first together, and he is also not by nature a particularly active man. He doesn't play sport or ride a bike and his work has always been rather sedentary – his jaw is the main part of his body to get a workout, because he spends so much of his time on the telephone. It's the nature of his business. By his mid-fifties his weight was completely out of control and blood tests indicated that his cholesterol was also creeping up. This was enough of a warning to give him a fright and make him start taking care of himself.

David's main form of exercise became power walking, which he has done every day of the year for about four years, for at least one and a half hours a day. It's part of his disciplined nature and I greatly admire the way he can stick to an exercise program once he gets going. It's almost impossible to get him to miss a day, no matter what other pressures may prevail or how terrible the weather. I can remember times when he went out for his power walk during heavy snow or driving sleet, such was his dedication to getting back into shape. It really worked too. In six months he shed nearly twenty kilos and looked and felt so much better. His general mood improved, his periods of depression disappeared and he was certainly much easier to live with. It was during this time that he started collecting those infuriating golf balls. He also joined the local fitness club, and after his walk he would swim laps of the pool and work out on the weight-lifting equipment. It worked fantastically. Not only did he lose all that weight, but his whole body shape changed as his muscle tone improved and he felt a lot better about himself. Instead of being irritable and lethargic, he became energetic and positive. It was a good time in our relationship.

In spite of this new-found fitness, in his late fifties he was diagnosed with mild late-onset diabetes. He had probably been borderline for years, which would explain his tendency to experience 'lows' during the day, periods when he could barely stay awake. These could happen anywhere, anytime: sitting waiting for traffic lights to change, while on the phone talking to business associates, in his comfortable armchair waiting for the seven o'clock news. This type of diabetes can be controlled by exercise, weight loss and sensible diet, which was a further incentive for him to keep on with his healthy routine.

During the six months I was overseas he was in Queensland making two films. His normal day-to-day living routine had to change to fit in with the pressures of film-making and, although he worked out during the weekends, the obsessive daily regime was disrupted. We came home after buying our house in France and he was hit by a nasty virus that left him feeling totally drained, physically and mentally. Over the next eighteen months he simply didn't exercise at all. His weight crept up and again he became despondent, depressed and obviously unhappy with the way he was looking and feeling. Diabetes can have a devastating effect on libido, and this side-effect began to manifest itself also. From being a man with a well-developed sex drive he gradually became uninterested – or so it appeared to me at the time. He seemed to switch off and, because I was not accustomed to being the one to initiate sexual contact, our relationship on this level petered out almost completely.

We have since talked a lot about this dark period of our relationship and it appears that it was more to do with a breakdown in communication between us than just the simple fact of David's diabetes destroying his libido. I had become a more critical and less patient wife, quick to admonish him for small irritations and possibly much less affectionate towards him. He took this change of attitude as a form of coolness and concluded that I wasn't very interested in him any more. At the same time I was lying in bed at night wondering what on earth had happened to our sex life.

It seems ridiculous that two people who have lived together for so long and know each other so well could slide so easily into this sort of misunderstanding. But at the time this was the case for both of us. He thought I didn't care for him any more and I thought he had lost interest in me. Our relationship was at an all-time low.

For David, order and routine are a sacred way of life. He is one of those obsessive individuals who rises at the same time every morning, and takes one hour to drink two cups of coffee and read the newspaper, and exactly twenty minutes to shower. He likes to eat exactly the same thing for breakfast every day, at the same time. He arranges his clothes in a certain order and wears them in sequence. Now he found himself in a strange house, with his routine completely in tatters and all sorts of practical problems to confront. The hot water system seemed dodgy and was heated by a wood-burning stove which was also the only oven for cooking. It didn't take long for the water to heat up – just an hour after lighting the stove with wood from the bush block at the back of the farm – but the taps and showers spurted and spluttered, one moment cascading boiling water, the next an icy cold stream. The water came from a spring that relied on a functioning pump. It was quite gritty, and muddy after rain. Some days the showers were dark brown, other days they turned the bathtubs and shower recesses green. The water system also relied on a pump that malfunctioned quite regularly. It had to be primed and there was a filter that needed to be routinely cleaned. Quite a change from our days of being on mains pressure and town water, where comfortable hot showers were as simple as the turn of a tap.

The farm was twenty-five minutes from Bathurst, so David felt that returning to the gym on a daily basis was an impractical and expensive proposition. Once again his weight began to creep up, as did the resulting feelings of despondency and depression. Our new lifestyle was much more challenging, and was complicated by the fact that David has never been a practical man. He has always left routine repairs and household maintenance to me, or we have paid a professional to solve problems. He has never really learned to cook or to manage tasks such as connecting up a hi-fi system or video player. At the farm we were living in relative isolation and had to cope with all the daily hassles as well as caring for the animals and the inevitable hardships and disasters of rural life. But David began to take on quite a few of the more tiresome domestic tasks of our everyday life. He enjoyed clearing up after meals, especially after dinner parties, and took the view that if I did all the cooking it was therefore his role to wash up and put away afterwards. He suddenly discovered the joys of shopping and became a canny bargain hunter; after decades of being the one to cart in boot-loads of groceries every week, I was now able to hand over this onerous task to him. His next triumph was mastering the washing machine and, this done, he took this boring chore completely off my shoulders (I think he was also sick of me losing his socks). But while he was now reasonably efficient around the house, mechanical or technical problems that arose were still greeted with panic.

If David was feeling unsettled by the move and his upended routine, he was soon about to feel a great deal worse. A week after arriving at the farm I abandoned him and went to France for a month. It was my first trip back since my glorious escape the previous year and it was to be the first time I would live in our village house. I planned to spend some time with Ethan and Lynne before they came back to Australia to have their baby, and to research and set up a walking tour around the villages in our region of France for the following year. I was filled with antici-pation and excitement; somehow the joy associated with moving to a new home, especially my longed-for farm, had totally eluded me. My mind and heart were already in France and the rest seemed like a dream.

David looked totally crestfallen as I climbed on board the small plane at Bathurst airport that would connect me to my flight to Toulouse. In so many ways I was relieved to be escaping from the chaos of the move, although I had managed to find the energy to unpack the pots and pans and set up the kitchen, to arrange the small living room and to make our bedroom as cosy and comfortable as possible. The rest of our possessions, including innumerable boxes of books, magazines, journals, clothes, paintings and family photographs, were still piled up in all directions. In truth, I was leaving David in the midst of a terrible mess and with the routine of his daily life in total disarray. I should have felt a little guilty, but I didn't. I had discovered the most exhilarating sense of freedom when I headed off for France last time, and this time was no different.

10

When I first arrive in Frayssinet-le-Gelat, Ethan and Lynne are in the process of packing up to return to Australia, although they still have one week to go, which means we can socialise together and give them a rousing farewell. They have become a popular young couple in the community and the locals have really taken them to heart. Lynne looks quite beautiful even though she is still feeling quite fragile; she has colour in her cheeks and that glorious glow that accompanies a happy pregnancy. Ethan seems to have grown up a lot, which is natural given the independence gained by travelling and working in a foreign country, not to mention impending fatherhood. He is not at all concerned about the actual birth, having been around during all Miriam's labours, with the exception of little Gus's. However, both he and Lynne have had to make a huge adjustment in not only accepting but embracing the idea of having a child while they are still in their early twenties. By the time I get to France they are filled with excitement and anticipation and it's good to see them so positive and happy.

They have done a lot of work on the house, painting the upstairs bedroom a crisp, clean white and cleaning out the attic room and finishing the walls with a thick, white render. They have also nested, making the house cosy and comfortable despite the lack of smart furniture and flash kitchen appliances. It looks well loved and well lived in, which is a vast difference from when we first bought it last December.

Our house is situated smack bang against the main road, with a narrow footpath, barely 45 centimetres wide, separating the front shutters from the rumbling wheels of passing trucks. Originally, the road would have been a relatively narrow dirt track, but progress has meant that all the winding country roads have been widened to accommodate the large trucks that hurtle through every day except Sunday, when there is a moratorium on heavy vehicle traffic. I suspect this national regulation is as much to do with preserving the age-old custom of the large family lunch on Sunday, for the sake of the truck drivers and their families, as much as for the ensuing peace on the road. Knowing that wine is often liberally consumed at these lengthy Sunday repasts, having no trucks on the road is also probably a sensible safety precaution.

The house is tall and narrow, with shutters on all three levels. It is no more than nine metres wide and it shares a wall with a more substantial house on the corner block. The remaining three walls are at least a metre thick, having been built using the traditional method of local stone with a mud slurry mortar. Late in the nineteenth century the front and side of the house were covered in crepi, a dull grey concrete-like render that became fashionable when the villagers tired of the sight of stone. The crepi was considered a neat and sophisticated finish, although these days it is deplored by new home owners who go to great lengths to chip away the render and reveal the gorgeous warm stonework that lies beneath.

Although the arched doorways that face the street still open, the main access is through a shuttered timber door on the side of the building. The large arched doors at the front are there because the house functioned as a shop over many generations, initially selling wooden agricultural baskets (trugs) that were made in the barn; in a later incarnation it was a hairdressing salon. There is evidence that the main downstairs room was once divided into two areas – the front portion being the shop and the back the living area for the family. This room would have been quite small, dominated by a huge stone fireplace, stone sink and a thick stone shelf used for food preparation. There would have been no space for any comfortable furniture, just a table and chairs; French families rarely had a sitting room or sofas. The constant cooking aromas and the warmth of the fire would have made the small room cosy and welcoming during winter, but unbearably hot and oppressive in summer when the July and August temperatures often hover for weeks in the high thirties.

The ceiling downstairs has been timber-lined, and my first inclination is to rip away the narrow boards to reveal the chunky timber beams that I am convinced are underneath. However, I am later discouraged by David, who feels it best to leave well enough alone. Uncovering anything unknown may lead to all sorts of disasters, not to mention the fact that the wiring and plumbing are all hidden inside this ceiling cavity. Heaven knows what we might find if we start ripping the room to pieces.

Some decades ago a back door was obviously excavated through the thick rear wall of the house, cutting the old stone washing up sink in half, sadly. This door leads out to the small square courtyard between the house and the barn. Unlike the rest of the house, the back wall has never been rendered with crepi, and the bare stone gives us a pretty good idea of how the house will look when we have chipped away at the front and side walls.

The ground-level floor is timber, but unfortunately it's very badly executed, a combination of narrow chestnut boards and mock timber sheeting laid over compressed board. Goodness knows what happened to the original oak flooring – I can only guess that at some stage a decision was made to raise or lower the floor level, and the cheapest option was taken. There's a cut-out square just inside the front door that looks like a trapdoor and, sure enough, when we jemmy it up we discover a cellar, or 'cave' as it's known in France, a must for any serious wine lover.

A handsomely curved timber stairway leads to the next floor, which consists of a small landing with a traditional window and shutters and two quite large but extremely plain bedrooms. The one facing the street has two windows, while the bedroom over-looking the courtyard has one window and a deep stone sink that no doubt served as the family bathroom in times gone by. Once again the floors are of chestnut and the boards are narrow, but fortunately it's all in good condition and quite authentic for the period of the house. This is the level I find most captivating.

The top level is reached on curved rickety stairs that are badly in need of replacement. There's plenty of headroom to the roof, but the beams are extraordinarily heavy and low – you have to duck your head to get from one area to the next. As usual, my first instinct is to remove the beams, but again expert advice indicates that this would be structural madness. The four thick stone walls are tied together by these massive beams and we would have to undertake major engineering work to create full headroom in the attic. I decide that we will think about it at a later stage and concentrate now on the two lower levels. Getting them comfortable and pretty will cost as much as we have in our limited budget.

The gravelled courtyard is backed by a two-storey stone barn, which for me is the most appealing part of the entire property. The door to the barn is original oak with heavy metal hinges, still very handsome and solid. Inside the darkness of the barn, which has no plumbing or electricity, there is the potential to create the most wonderful extra bedroom and bathroom, and perhaps even an office if I ever decide to spend a year in France writing another book. The first time I stood inside the barn I contemplated what it might have been used for at various times – perhaps chickens and a cow, or even a couple of pigs. The concept of living in such close proximity to large animals in a confined space is fairly revolting, but it was probably the norm in villages like this for centuries.

The least attractive aspect of the house is the bathroom, added along the back wall probably thirty years ago. It is an ugly concrete-block corridor that has been rendered on the outside with stucco and badly tiled on the inside. It's gloomy, damp and cold, and definitely needs rethinking if we are to make the house comfortable for long-term visits.

In spite of its shortcomings, the house is quite livable in a basic way, and we were lucky enough to buy it with all the furniture and furnishings thrown in by its former English owners. Although we plan to gradually replace everything, it is handy not to have to go out and buy items like vacuum cleaners, clothes dryers and tables and chairs. When we first move in all we require is some basic linen. There is no central heating, which locals insist is essential if you plan to stay in France for a full year, but there is a fully functional cast-iron Godin slow-combustion stove in the fireplace, which I light almost immediately after we arrive.

Ignoring the fine details and the work that has to be done some time in the future, the house has an innately charming atmosphere and an appeal that is very plain, very French and very rural. At home I would never contemplate buying a house on a main road, but somehow in this French village it feels perfect. All the houses that adjoin the main intersection and the square that surrounds the Romanesque Church are in the same position as us, right on the road, and it's as though we share the same living situation. Our neighbours on the high side are M and Mme Thomas, an elderly couple with a house clad in drab grey crepi just like ours. Their daughter and son-in-law live in the adjoining house, with two teenage sons who travel each day into Prayssac by bus to the high school. The Thomases have a walled garden just up the road, overflowing with produce and flowers. There are fruiting trees and vines, neat rows of lettuce and various greens, and in summer enough tomatoes to feed the two families all year round. Climbing roses and clematis drip from the stone walls surrounding the garden, and hidden at the back of the house is a modern swimming pool for summer dipping.

Within a day of my return my diary is filled with a series of catching-up lunches and dinners and I realise that I am bound to fall back into my bad old habits – lingering lunches at Mme Murat's, hazy afternoon sleeps to recover, followed by equally filling evening meals in the company of friends. Not the healthiest of lifestyles, but one that I can't help but enjoy. I wonder, if I were living here full-time would I be a little more circumspect? Cut back the socialising and lead a more balanced and sensible life? Jock doesn't, and I fear that I would probably be just like him. Heaven help my waistline!

I still can't believe it's ten months since I was last here. I am so excited to come back and renew my many good friendships, the connections that bound me during my first visit and helped convince me that I should make France a permanent part of my life. My first friend in the Lot was Jock, a retired journalist and larger-than-life character in every sense of the phrase. When I wrote about my adventures in rural France I described Jock as the 'King of Grunge' because of his dishevelled appearance and penchant for red wine, the dregs of which often decorate the front of his shirt. My picture of his appearance and lifestyle draws roars of recognition from all who know him, but Jock steadfastly refuses to acknowledge this unanimous public perception. An advance copy of the book arrives a few days after my return and, after reading it, he lets me off lightly.

'I told you that you could say whatever you wanted about me, as long as it wasn't the truth. And because I am not the drunken, noisy slob you have portrayed in your book, I can't possibly take offence.'

Thank heavens for his self-deprecating sense of humour. Jock generally refuses to acknowledge reality and drifts through life with a blind optimist's adoration of his much loved little patch of the world. Perhaps he's indicative of men in general, who cannot really see themselves as dispassionately as the rest of the world (especially women) see them. A medical survey carried out a few years ago tested individual perceptions about weight and appearance. Most men, no matter what their size and shape, had a view of themselves as being quite slim and in good shape. They looked at their peers and commented on how they had 'aged' but couldn't actually see themselves as being in the same boat. Women, on the other hand, no matter how slender, complained of looking unattractive and of being overweight. They worried at the first sign of aging and generally had a critical view of themselves.

Inside Jock's large, mid-seventy-year-old body there beats the heart of a man much younger and more energetic. He still sees himself as being about thirty years old, rakishly attractive (which he still is, of course) and with a constitution that can effortlessly tolerate a wild and often hedonistic lifestyle. He must have been blessed with a fantastic set of genes and a cast-iron constitution, but he also has certain medically based limitations – lungs that wheeze and splutter after more than seven decades of chronic asthma and a heart that has successfully undergone major surgery and should be treated with a little more respect.

Jock's main problem is that he is such a popular and entertaining guest that his summer diary is crammed with invitations for lunches, dinners, drinks and general merriment. All his friends worry about him because from time to time his entire system falls apart, and on at least two occasions he has ended up in hospital with a life-threatening illness, the last one pneumonia. However, it takes more than a little brush with death to stop Jock in his tracks, and after a week of slowing down to recover he's back on deck, ready to party.

The contrasts in Jock's life are profound. During the long,

hot days of summer he is on a non-stop treadmill of social activities, with house guests and parties that stretch for weeks into months. He gains a lot of weight, becomes even more florid in the face and often looks as though he's been to hell and back a few times. In winter the entire social scene calms down and, as temperatures plummet to below zero, Jock hibernates in his small stone house, often remaining in his study, where the only heater is, before wandering into the icy kitchen to cook up some dinner or up to his equally frosty bedroom to sleep. He attempts to brighten this dreary winter hiatus by throwing the odd dinner party – he's an excellent and creative cook – but friends attend with some trepidation. A mutual friend recounts sitting through a delicious four-course dinner wearing her overcoat, scarf and gloves; others claim they furiously stoke the fire but still shiver all night. Last winter his oldest friends, Margaret and Lucience, ganged up and insisted that he install some electric heaters. However, Jock is still inclined to absent-mindedly leave a door or window open, so it's never cosy.

In summer Jock reverts to his wild ways, exhausting by association all those within his orbit. It's not uncommon for him to attend a lunch that lingers on until five o'clock, go home for a snooze then out again to an evening meal or party that starts at 7.30 and goes until well after midnight. Concerned about his health, I once emailed him from Australia saying that I had heard via the grapevine that he had been 'overdoing it' a little, considering he was not long out of hospital. He replied with an amusing slice of his diary, detailing his various social activities, ending each one with 'and woke the following morning feeling absolutely fine'. Well, perhaps Jock's idea of 'fine' is different from most people's. I know how I feel after a few weeks trying to keep up with his pace in France, and 'fine' isn't the word. It's 'ruined'!

Like everyone living in a remote rural region, Jock is totally dependent on his car for mobility. There are no taxis or trains or buses in the countryside so, after a five-hour lunch, driving home, no matter in what condition, is unavoidable. Over time Jock's reliable old Peugeot has taken a bit of a battering. The rubber side-strips have been scraped off, one by one. The side mirrors have been known to take out the odd passing shrub, and the back bumper bar has born the brunt of more than half a dozen badly judged reverses. The driver-side front fender is entirely caved in, though Jock insists he wasn't responsible for that one – someone backed into him in a car park. And there's a running gag among his friends about a 'Watch Out For Children' sign erected in the driveway of a friend's rental house: Jock has knocked it down at least four times.

His worst accident happened one summer when he attended a morning drinks party that somehow became a lunch party that somehow continued with glasses of wine into the early evening. Jock suddenly realised the lateness of the hour and decided he should go home, weaving his car down the long driveway, pruning some of the hedge with his side mirrors. Next morning his neighbours were horrified to see his badly dented car parked out the front of his house. The passenger side was completely stoved in and the front bumper bar was on the road. Mid-morning, Jock emerged from his house a little rumpled and red-faced but none the worse for wear. He seemed highly amused, revealing that as he pulled in to park in front of his house, his foot 'slipped' off the brake and the car plunged forward into the thick stone front wall. The car was pronounced 'totalled' by the local mechanic, M Moliere, and without insurance Jock was faced with having to rustle up the funds for a new one. When asked by friends what had happened, Jock responded in characteristic fashion: 'The front wall reared up and attacked the car,' he said.

Meanwhile, back in Australia, all is not running smoothly down on the farm. David is feeling a profound sense of loneliness and disconnection, not having me there to soothe his passage into our new environment. He has befriended our rather eccentric neighbour Russell, who pops over the fence for a beer and a chat about local life in the district. Like David, Russell is a hoarder, except that his collections consist mainly of junk which is scattered at random from one end of his property to the other. There are rusting sheets of corrugated iron, old water tanks riddled with holes, kitchen and laundry appliances, sinks, baths, toilets, buckets, and piles of railway sleepers and tangled coils of wire. You could be forgiven for thinking that his side paddock is the local tip, only probably not as tidy. In and around the drifts of rubbish Russell manages to cultivate organic vegetables mainly leeks and rhubarb for the commercial market, and has a large flock of honking geese that he allows to graze and keep the grass down. There are two old houses on the property but Russell actually lives in the shed. The houses are rented out to augment his meagre income. But Russell is strangely lovable and David grows immediately fond of him, looking forward to his spontaneous afternoon visits that help break the silence.

As the weeks pass David discovers various practical problems around the property, a pretty normal occurrence when you move to somewhere new. The water pump frequently malfunctions, leaving him mid-shower with his customary head-to-toe soapy lather and suddenly no water to rinse it off. Neighbours come to the rescue, helping to prime the pump and get things moving again, at least for a day or so.

The animals are also taking time to adjust to the new place. Floyd, our half-blind Labrador, disappears for hours at a time and David worries that he may wander as far as the highway, where he could be skittled or, worse, cause a terrible accident. Searching for him one day, he encounters a half-naked elderly man in one of Russell's rented cottages who introduces himself as Frank. He has a thick Dutch accent and a broad sense of humour.

'Have you seen a Labrador?' David asks.

'Sure I have,' says Frank. 'He was here two minutes ago and killed one of the geese.'

David reels back in disbelief and becomes instantly defensive.

'That couldn't have been our Floyd,' he stammers. 'Floyd has grown up with chickens and ducks. He loves poultry. He would *never ever* kill a bird. He's a Labrador.'

Frank roars with laughter. 'And I'm a fucking Dutchman. Don't worry about it. I hate those bloody geese. I hope your Labrador comes back and kills the rest of them.'

David slinks off and eventually Floyd returns looking quite innocent, no traces of blood or feathers around his mouth.

The cats have been allocated the laundry to settle in, but eventually David starts to let them have the run of the house and garden. Disoriented, they immediately start messing in the corners and he rings Miriam in alarm.

'The cats have crapped on the carpet,' he reports in some disgust.

'Well, clean it up,' she says with little compassion. As the mother of four small boys, her life is a constant round of bum wiping and associated mess, and she has little time for her father and his helplessness.

The cats are banned from the house until I return and some semblance of normal life is restored.

Mid-October the weather suddenly turns bitterly cold and there is a black frost that burns the tips off every tree and shrub in the garden. The wind howls across the paddocks and buffets the house in icy blasts. David isn't very good at keeping the fires going and the atmosphere is bleak and dreary.

Already prone to depression, during this period alone at the farm he falls into a black hole. When I phone him from France, bubbling with excitement about living in the house in Frayssinet and catching up with all my friends, the intrigues of village life and the joys of the local food, he sounds totally down in the dumps and negative.

'Don't you like it there?' I ask with some degree of guilt.

'Not really,' he says. 'It's cold and the house is very large and very empty. I wish I was back in Leura.'

My heart sinks at this news. I am beginning to feel that I have pushed for too much change in too short a time. Not only have I insisted on buying this little village house so that I can escape to it every year, I have also uprooted David from our home at Leura so that when I am away he is living in unfamiliar surroundings. Yet I also feel unreasonably irritated by his inability to adapt and cope. After all, Miriam, Rick and his four grandsons are only twenty-five minutes away by car and he can easily spend more time with them if he's feeling lonely or down. In the back of my mind is always the niggling resentment from years gone by.

He repeatedly left me to cope with a large house and four young children for months at a time, and now it's my turn. It's not that I don't feel some compassion for his predicament, it's just that I am determined to hang on to this precious time when I can be my own person.

Just before Ethan and Lynne catch the plane back to Australia for the birth of their baby a surprise party is held in their honour – a combined farewell and baby shower. Our English friend Carole organises the party, collecting money for a present for the baby – an elaborate and very stylish French baby carriage that includes a car capsule for a newborn. I drive Ethan and Lynne to Bob and Carole's, ostensibly for a farewell drink. A crowd of twenty-five friends have gathered and they leap forward as we enter, much to the kids' astonishment. Lynne is over-whelmed by the generosity of her new friends and sheds a few tears. She and Ethan spend hours working out how the various components of the pram slot together. It's great that they have been accepted into this community but also sad that they can't stay and have their baby here at the local hospital. At a time like this, Lynne needs her family's support, and they would not be covered by the French health system, which would make it a very expensive delivery.

A few days later I drive them to Toulouse airport and as they book in at the Air France counter we realise that the folded pram has now put them seriously overweight in the baggage depart-ment. They are slapped with a massive excess baggage bill and the young woman behind the counter doesn't show a flicker of compassion despite the fact that Lynne is obviously distressed. I offer to pay the bill with my credit card, reassuring them that they can repay me with some work at the farm when I get back.

I laugh quietly to myself, thinking it would have been cheaper for me to buy them a pram at home, but of course they are so thrilled with the stylish French one that it's unthinkable not to take it back.

Back at the house, I am alone within those four thick stone walls for the first time. I light a fire, put on some music and pour a glass of wine, soaking up the mood and trying to regain the heady feeling I had the previous year of being a woman living alone in a small French village. It's an overwhelmingly seductive sensation. I feel rather decadent being so free and independent, sparing barely a thought for David at home, trying to settle into the farm and feeling so lonely without me.

After a day or two of just revelling in the delights of the house I start to get organised for the real purpose of this visit – setting up the village walking tours that I aim to run every year to justify my annual visit. My friend Jan, originally from New Zealand and now living full-time in France with her French landscaper husband Philippe, has agreed to help me with the task, which involves booking hotels and bus companies and working out an interesting and varied itinerary. Her French language skills are terrific and we set off to visit all the towns in the region to gather material from each one's Office de Tourisme. I have decided that walking should be an important facet of the tour; it's by far the best way of seeing the local countryside and appreciating its unique beauty.

During this period of setting up the tour I ponder the rights and wrongs of bringing Australian tourists to regional France. After all, I have just experienced the downside of tourism in my home village back in Australia, so I question whether it is absurd of me to be doing exactly the same in reverse here in our quiet little region of France. I run my doubts past our friends, asking them how they feel about my bringing Australian tourists to the Lot.

'Don't worry about it,' says Jock. 'It will be fun. As long as I can still get a seat at Madame Murat's restaurant, I have no objections.'

'It will be a boost to the local economy,' says Jan. 'It will provide some work for the bus companies and income for the hotels. It's a great idea.'

'You just can't have too many Australians,' says my English friend Miles, wryly.

I feel slightly reassured that I am not turning the Lot into Disneyland, but I still wonder whether the local French population, those not directly involved in or benefiting from tourism, will be as enthusiastic. I can only hope that the fact that the tours are very small (fewer than twenty people) and infrequent (twice a year at most) will lessen their impact on the quiet lifestyle of this region. And I hope that because things here are usually very quiet, the locals will regard the arrival of a few Australians as entertaining rather than irritating. My doubts about this issue are not allayed when we start to make contacts.

Jan and I decide we need to investigate hotels, so that we can calculate just how many people we can accommodate. This is very much rural France and the hotels are quite limited in size and room numbers. I am expecting hotel owners to fall over themselves with delight when we tell them we are planning to bring a tour group to their establishments, but nothing is further from the truth. The first hotelier we meet, at Gourdon, looks askance at the suggestion.

'But we have a very select clientele,' he informs Jan. 'I am not sure that we would want a large group of Australians staying at our hotel.'

Even though Jan is acting as the translator, my French is good enough to understand exactly what he is saying, and his arrogant, curled-lip attitude causes me great amusement. I should have realised that the French are not always totally enthused about tourism, even though it is such a vital part of their economy. We decide to give this particular hotel a big miss.

Fortunately, not all the hoteliers are as snooty, and over a period of two weeks we piece together an itinerary that includes daily walks and picnic lunches, visits to farms and vineyards, chateaux and gardens, a boat trip down the River Lot and some of the best evening meals that food lovers could wish for. Jan and I also prepare by doing some of the proposed walks, using both French and English guidebooks that detail scenic tours in the region. This doesn't prove as easy as it looks, because the guidebooks give cryptic and often contradictory instructions. We enjoy a walk from Bouziers to the picturesque town of St Cirq Lapopie, an ancient village that hovers dramatically over the Lot River. The walk takes us along the river's edge, with overhanging cliffs and romantic scenery. On the way back we decide to walk a different route. The guidebook tells us to 'turn left at the chicken house'. We can't find any sort of structure for housing fowls so we take a right-hand turn and proceed gaily along, not realising that we are walking many kilometres away from the river. After an hour or more it becomes obvious that we have gone completely wrong and we retrace our footsteps. It takes all afternoon to find our way back to Bouziers, where we left the car. We laugh uproariously at our ineptitude, both hoping that when and if we do get a tour group together we will not get them so thoroughly lost and exhausted. We quickly realise that there's a lot of work involved in setting up a tour itinerary – it's not just a matter of taking some casual strolls or making a few phone calls.

There's quite a difference between living in the Lot full-time and being a part-time holiday resident. It's a bit like the difference between a full-time marriage and a holiday romance. Those who live here all year round have to deal with the day-to-day frustration of French bureaucracy, the ups and downs of the climate, the idiosyncrasies of the neighbours and the fact that during the winter months life here can be both bleak and boring. For those of us who drift in and out during the height of the season when the days are long and the twilights balmy, the reality of being a full-time French resident simply doesn't impinge.

There are certainly problems for people who are not here all year: things can go wrong when there is nobody around taking care of the premises. When Jock goes away, which he rarely does these days, he never even locks the front door because he doesn't own a key. Even if he did have a key he probably wouldn't bother, because he is the least security-minded individual on the planet. People whose houses are in more isolated situations do have security problems when the houses are left empty for long periods. Another couple I know, who generally only visit their converted barn for one month a year, close it up securely with heavy timber shutters and hefty metal hinges. They have planted a tall hedge along the road front; this has the advantage of screening the traffic noise and visual pollution, but also blocks the view of the house from the neighbouring farms and thus makes it more vulnerable to robbery. Last summer a neighbouring farmer noticed a van parked outside the front door. Knowing that the house was not meant to be occupied for at least the next three months, he walked over to investigate. As he approached, two men leapt into the van and took off at high speed. The contents of the van – electronic bits and pieces and furniture from the house – were later found dumped in a field and restored to their rightful owners, who were lucky that their neighbours were so vigilant.

The little house in the woods, where I lived for four months in the year 2000, was also targeted because of its isolation and the fact that the owners only visit once or twice every year. Like a lot of holiday houses, there was nothing much of value inside, but the outside barn was raided and tools, both garden and workshop, were removed. In the end the owners strung chains to the chestnut trees to prevent cars or vans being driven on site, and paid a local man to make random visits to keep an eye on things.

During winter in this region temperatures sink well below zero, sometimes as low as minus fifteen degrees, and home owners experience terrible plumbing problems with frozen toilets and pipes that seize up, expand and burst, even inside the thick stone walls. Part-time residents must be careful to turn off their water at the mains and drain hot water tanks and kitchen and bathroom taps to make sure there is no water left in the pipes that might create havoc while they are not in residence. During my first winter I dutifully turned off the water and drained the tank, but neglected to drain the tap to the bathroom sink, leaving a residue of water in the pipe. During January it froze and split the pipe under the sink. Because the water was off there was no damage and the problem was detected as soon as Ethan switched on the water when he and Lynne arrived. I have been told horror stories about burst pipes that have cascaded water inside bathrooms and down into cellars for weeks or even months before the owners returned for their holiday to find total devastation (not to mention a mind-boggling water bill).

Australia has various native animals, possums in particular, that drive home owners to distraction by taking up residence in the roof cavity and clumping around all night in mating, nesting and child-rearing rituals. In France the equivalent ceiling-dwelling beast is larger and more unpleasant. The pine marten (*Martes* spp.) is a mammal about the size of a domestic cat with dense, chocolate-brown or grey-brown fur that is highly prized for making fashionable coats, which is why their numbers have dwindled across the northern hemisphere over the centuries. Some species are commonly known as sable, and their fur is as valuable as mink. They are all members of the weasel family and are very shy, rarely moving into open spaces and most likely to be seen at night. Their natural habitat is woodland areas, although they are very attracted to quiet, deserted houses. If they can find a way into the dry, protected space between ceiling and roof, they will certainly set up a nest. Unlike possums, who are herbi-vorous, martens are mostly carnivores, eating small birds and other mammals such as mice and rats as well as berries, birds' eggs, fungi, insects and carrion. They hunt over a wide territory but invariably return to the place of their birth with their prey. They have three or four offspring a year and can live for many years – more than a decade if there are no predators, such as foxes, to keep their numbers down.

In theory they are protected animals: in the UK they are classified as an endangered species and there are laws to protect them. In France they are also protected but there is a much more ruthless disregard for their well-being should they invade human territory. Our Frayssinet neighbours, Anne and Miles Rotherham, who spend most of the year in London, returned one summer to the sound and distinctive smell of a family of martens living in the roof. The ceilings were stained from their urine and faeces and there was an overpowering smell of rotting eggs because the martens had been raiding the local birds' nests and chicken runs and returning to their roof nest with vast collections of eggs to store for later consumption. They have vicious teeth, making them virtually impossible to catch. Philippe, the gardener, was badly mauled trying to grab one and has nurtured an abiding loathing for them ever since.

How to dispose of unwanted martens is a topic of lively conversation in the local bar, with various grisly solutions being proposed by shopkeepers and members of the chasse, the hunters who bound through the woods from autumn to spring taking potshots at boar, deer and hare (and each other) on a regular basis. In French martens are called fouine and there is even a verb, fouiner, which roughly translates as 'to pry inquisitively' or 'nose about'. It captures the sly, nosy character of these creatures, and every local has an anecdote or theory on how they can best be discouraged – although it never seems to involve catching them and relocating them to a more sympathetic environment. The most popular eradication process involves lacing eggs with strychnine and leaving them in places where the martens will discover and devour them. The trick is to prevent them taking the lethal eggs back into the roof, for after eating these eggs the martens will promptly die and decompose, causing even more intense odours and ceiling staining. Miles relies on the local head of the chasse, who is reputed to have great success in this area. He injects the eggs with poison and hides them around the garden, then waits for the martens to emerge. Once they are out, their lofty entrance is blocked securely and then it's just a matter of waiting for the strychnine to take effect. The corpses are found in the garden several days later and, for reasons unknown to me, buried deep in Anne's impressive compost and manure heap. I know this for a fact because some months later I am helping Anne plant seedlings around their rambling garden and I decide to grab a barrowload of compost to spread as a mulch. Thrusting my hand deeply into the sweetly fragrant pile of rich organic matter I suddenly encounter a very different texture – something warm and slimy envelops my hand to the wrist. As I quickly pull back a smell overpowers me. Anne is most apologetic.

'I think Philippe and Miles buried the dead fouines in the compost,' she explains.

I'm sure they smell frightful when nesting in the roof, piddling and copulating all over the ceiling. But they smell even worse when festering in the compost. I'm glad to say these are the only martens I have so far encountered in France.

The more time I spend in France, the more opportunity I have to establish relaxed relationships with those locals I see on a daily basis. It's difficult when language sets up such an impenetrable barrier, but my vocabulary has improved to the extent that I can participate in simple conversations, peppered with a lot of hand actions and general meaningless laughter. There are two bars now operating in the village. I usually frequent the one closest to the house – Le Relais, which loosely translates as 'staging post'. It is similar to the old inns scattered around the Australian countryside where travellers stopped and rested on their long, dusty journeys.

The owners of the bar are Christian and Christiane, and they set the tone for the establishment both in their appearance and demeanour. Christian is in his fifties, and has a face that is no doubt a testament to a lifetime of heavy smoking and fairly devoted wine consumption. He can, at first meeting, appear rather gruff, but once he has decided you are okay, he breaks into a ready smile and enjoys a little frivolous banter. I discover after all this time that he can speak quite a bit of English, a fact he has kept well hidden from me – and, I guess, from most of his other English-speaking customers. The bar opens early, about nine o'clock, and locals pop in for a steaming coffee, usually bringing a croissant or pain au chocolat from the nearby patisserie. By ten o'clock some of the harder cases are starting to scuttle into the bar, drinking pastis or red wine well before the church bell is rung at midday, the usual signal that it's okay to have an aperitif prior to a hearty lunch. If I have been working hard in the morning, writing or painting or chipping crepi off the exterior walls, I answer the call of the bell and wander down for a pre-lunch drink or two. If it's hot, I order a pression, the local draught beer, which is excellent. On colder days I join the craggy-faced locals in a pastis. The bar is very dark and could be described as depressing if you were not genuinely captivated by its dingy, smoky atmosphere. Once inside, my eyes adjust and I see Christian, cigarette in hand, behind the bar. He starts his customary running joke.

'Bonjour, Marie, ça va?' as we cordially shake hands.

'Voulez-vous un café ou un jus d'orange?' laughing at his own ironic reference to my preference for something a little stronger.

If the weather is good I take my drink out onto the footpath or across the road, where Christian has set up tables, chairs and umbrellas in the forecourt area of the ancient church. This is a great way of being spotted by friends driving home from work for their two or three-hour lunch break. They furiously beep their klaxon (horn), or call out rude remarks about my predilection for drinking beer in a public place at midday. Or, more frequently, they stop and join me for an aperitif or two. These chance encounters can be a bit of a trap, especially if I am spied by one of the more enthusiastic drinkers in the group. Several times I have found myself not getting back to the house for lunch until two o'clock, by which time I have lost all interest in eating and am more likely to lie down for a nap instead.

Only during lunchtime, when the drivers have stopped for their well-earned two-hour feast, does the village become silent. The rest of the time trucks pass closely enough for the drinkers to reach out and touch them as they rumble by, belching out clouds of diesel and rarely slowing down much, in spite of the approaching dangerous intersection. In high summer, groups of youths gather in the afternoon to drink beer and some actually position their plastic chairs in the roadway so that the trucks are forced to drive around them. This is alarming for me to observe, but the young men don't bat an eyelid. They obviously have confidence that the truck drivers won't risk not making their delivery deadline by running over a pedestrian (not that you can really call someone sitting on a chair in the road a pedestrian).

Le Relais also serves food at lunch and dinner time: a simple three courses which includes a plat that is generally either steak au frites or poulet au frites. They make excellent potage (soup) and always offer dessert. You can get basic sandwiches of jambon au fromage, served on crispy white baguettes with lots of creamy butter. The food is prepared by Christiane, who is possibly in her early forties, slim with a pretty face and a warm disposition. Unlike her husband, she always greets me with two kisses, and by my third visit she is attempting to speak to me in English by saying 'Hello, Marie' whenever I enter the bar. I decide that hello isn't really ideal for an Australian greeting and teach her to say 'Gidday' with a broad Aussie accent. She is intrigued, and within a few weeks several of the regulars also adopt this casual greeting, laughing heartily at the oddness of the word. There doesn't seem to be a single word in French that sounds even vaguely similar.

I gather that Christian and Christiane have both been married before. Christian has a son in his early twenties by a previous relationship, a handsome young man by the name of Giles, who seems to have most of the young women in the village drooling over him. Giles rarely rises before midday, and then comes into the bar for a heart-starting short black coffee, oozing with that 'just rolled out of the sack' appearance. Indeed, I notice that in the French cosmetic salons it is possible to buy a hair gel or mousse that creates the dishevelled appearance of someone who has just emerged from their bed and not bothered to brush their hair. I suppose it's meant to be sexy, and it certainly works for Giles if you consider the number of gorgeous young women who hover around him! Giles works in the afternoons at the local 'Quad Hire', a summer holiday tourist attraction where visitors hire four-wheel bikes, grotesque-looking machines with wheels as big as a tractor's. They roar around the woodland tracks and the back blocks of local farms, making an outrageous amount of noise and causing general disruption; all this is tolerated as the normal summer madness of rural France. Giles has a dog who follows him around wearing the same baleful expression as most of the young women. A leggy brown and white hunting dog called Alf, he often sits in the road so that the truck drivers have to avoid him as well as the beer drinkers. It's all very casual.

Christian and Christiane also have a ten-year-old son, Guillaume . In between cooking meals and serving drinks, Christiane helps him with his homework in the late afternoon, sitting at one of the tables surrounded by the jolly noise of the drinkers. The attitude to children in bars here is certainly much more casual than in Australia. Children tend to wander in and out, looking for their parents, and it's not uncommon to see young women with babies sitting in the bar during the daytime. Indeed, a rather plump young mother with a three month-old baby comes every day for several hours; while the baby is sleeping or gurgling happily in its pram, the mother drinks coffee after coffee and smokes cigarettes. It seems a terrific antidote to the loneliness and isolation of new motherhood – she chats and shares a joke with the locals who come and go, especially during the middle of the day when the shops close for two hours and their owners pop in for a quick aperitif. However, I wonder about the smoky, dingy atmosphere in which the baby is spending so much time – locals actually bend over the pram to goo and gaa at the gorgeous little chap, exhaling smoke fumes as they admire his progress.

This cavalier attitude towards health and safety issues is very typical of France. There is a general dislike of rules and regulations and, while Australians accept strict 'No Smoking' rules in hotels, restaurants and airports and on public transport, this simply would not be tolerated in France. Sitting on the train to Toulouse one day I am engulfed by fumes from a young woman in the seat in front of me, who chain-smokes the entire way. The moment passengers tumble from the plane into the airport terminal building, clouds of cigarette smoke surround the travellers, who are not obliged to wait until they get out into the fresh air. Bars and restaurants are never smoke-free zones and parents can often be seen smoking inside cars with the windows up and children in the back seat. The same attitude permeates other aspects of French life. While seatbelts are mandatory, they are often not fastened, especially around toddlers and small children. Bike riders don't wear helmets, and road and parking restrictions are gleefully ignored.

Part of me admires this anarchic behaviour, but the more conservative side of me worries that children, who are often the victims of it, will suffer without having any say.

Most days at Le Relais there is also a young local man, Pascal, who scurries about collecting glasses, wiping tables and carrying drink orders across the road, dodging the trucks without spilling a drop. Pascal has a slightly odd look about him and drives one of those tiny 'lawnmower engine' cars that are sold in France to people who can't get a regular driver's licence. You see a lot of old people who may have failed their test because of poor eyesight driving to the markets and back in these boxy little vehicles which, I have been told, are hugely expensive and quite tricky to drive because of their odd gearing. However, because of their low horsepower and their inability to reach a speed of more than 40 km/h, they have become a popular vehicle for people who would otherwise not qualify to be on the road. I figure that Pascal has some kind of disability, which is probably also why he has been given semi-permanent work at the bar. It's a common attitude in rural France to try to find useful occupations for people who may otherwise not be employable. The church bell-ringer, for example, is unable to hear or speak but has great prestige in the village because of his daily ringing of the bell at midday and dusk. I admire the inclusive and accepting attitude of the local community.

It is a curious concept that unlicensed drivers are allowed on the road in flimsy vehicles, no matter how underpowered. Drivers disqualified for repeated drink-driving offences could easily be out there too, but the attitude to such 'misdemeanours' is much more casual in France. Even though there is a fear of being caught, it seldom happens. The simple truth, however, is that the road statistics in rural France, especially here in the southwest, are appalling, with more deaths and injuries per capita than anywhere in Europe. It's a sobering thought.

12

Even though I am busy setting up the tour, I have time to stop and think about my life back in Australia compared with my life as a single woman here. I have been wishing that I had more time here this year, but pressures of work and moving from the Leura house to the farm have impinged and I am due back in October for the release of *Au Revoir*. This is a daunting prospect because I have been so candid in the writing of the book, exposing my life – and the lives of my family members – to close scrutiny. Although I worked in television for almost a decade, wandering around on camera in a straw hat pruning the roses, it is a very different matter to write a book that reveals intimate memories and feelings.

I am also worrying about my future with David at the farm, and I am wondering if the move was such a good idea after all. Faced with the prospect of being alone out on the farm with him day after day – as we are now both working from home offices – I seriously wonder if I will be able to cope with his melancholic disposition. It's many years since I last seriously contemplated the fact that my marriage could be in trouble, but I am starting to think that perhaps my desire to leave him and come to France for extended periods is just the beginning of the end.

I start to fantasise about being a single woman again, perhaps living here in France full-time, working as a writer and only going home to visit my children and grandchildren once a year. A lot of people do it – a lot of people live in foreign countries and only see their family from time to time. A lot of people also end their marriage after thirty years for reasons not dissimilar to the issues I am facing. Our children are all grown up now and independent – surely the separation or divorce of their parents could not be traumatic at this stage of the game?

In my heart I know this isn't true. Our children would be just as distressed if we were to part now as they would have been if it had happened when they were little children, perhaps even more so. A marriage isn't simply the union of two people for life. It's a complex relationship that involves all the people that surround it and are part of it – our children and their partners, our grandchildren and extended families, our friends. What we have created over the years isn't to be treated lightly, even if I am struggling at this stage to remain happy within the boundaries of the relationship. Part of me thinks that I should stop worrying about everyone else and how they feel and seize the day, striking out for my own personal happiness no matter what the consequences. And the other part of me knows perfectly well that I could never be really happy living away from the large family unit that we have created.

When I was first in France I met and socialised with a lot of interesting men – married men, divorced men, retired men, tradesmen, men who had never married, men who had had a succession of girlfriends, Frenchmen, Englishmen, New Zealanders, Americans, Canadians. As men or as potential lovers, I didn't really give them a second thought at the time – except sometimes in disturbing dreams that I realise now, with hindsight, I can attribute to the hormonal fluctuations of my impending menopause. I have always thrived in the company of men, especially en masse. It's not that I don't adore my female friends – most women I know have positive qualities that far outshine those of their husbands or boyfriends or lovers. But I have always loved being surrounded by men.

When I was a teenage girl, I had a small 'gang' of boys that I used to hang out with instead of the usual gaggle of girlfriends. These boys, many of whom I still keep in regular contact with today, were spotty and lanky and in most cases going through that awkward stage of life when young women were unavailable to them, so they seemed delighted that I was prepared to sneak out of my bedroom window at night to meet up with them and share their nocturnal adventures. Initially there was nothing sexual in my relationship with these boys, although I am sure there was a constant undercurrent of sexual tension that I found exciting. But there is safety in numbers, and being the only girl in a gang of eight or ten boys had its own in-built feeling of security. To be honest, I just loved being the sole female at the centre of this odd assortment of young blokes.

I didn't have to compete with other girls for attention – and I could flirt to my heart's content, knowing that I had them wound round my little finger. It was also a reflection of how I felt about myself physically. With a shock of curly red hair, a face full of freckles and a pear-shaped body, I believed myself to be totally unattractive. My voluptuous and more sophisticated girlfriends were all blondes with rich golden-honey tans and smooth fringes and they looked ravishing in their brief bikinis, sunning themselves at the beach. My skin went from snowy white to painful red in the sun, while my freckles darkened and joined together to form deep brown blotches. After a swim my hair sprang into a frizzy tangle, and I was incapable of filling the bra cup of any swimming costume. Psychologists would no doubt say that as a teenager I suffered low self-esteem. I just felt rather plain, which is why I avoided being seen out and about with the gorgeous girls and hung out with the spotty boys instead.

My way of relating to these young men was to become one of them. I wanted to be one of the blokes. I could drink as many beers (often more), smoke as many cigarettes, puff on as many joints, swear and tell rude jokes with the same enthusiasm and even partake of some of the risk-taking behaviour that young men seem to enjoy – driving recklessly in fast cars after an all-night party and walking a fine line between honesty and breaking the law.

I expect that my behaviour during my teens was also connected with my unhappy home life. The atmosphere in the house was far from harmonious, and tensions between my parents made me crave the fun and excitement I enjoyed when in the company of my gang. I really don't know how I survived my last few years at school. I got very little sleep as a result of our nocturnal roamings; it was not uncommon for me to sneak back home at 4 am, sleep for three hours, then get up and get ready for school. We always managed to scrape together enough money to buy beer, so most days I was not only exhausted but slightly hung-over. Not a recipe for academic achievement!

Eventually, after a couple of years, I did become sexually involved with one of these boys and we ended up living together in a group house for almost three years. But this was all before I met David and started down the long road of our thirty-one-year relationship.

There's a lot to be said for a younger woman having a sexual relationship with an older and more experienced man. When David and I first got together I was very unworldly and unadventurous when it came to lovemaking. In those early years he opened me up to the joy and passion of a healthy sexual relationship and it was this, I often used to joke, that kept our marriage together when times were tough. Our children were always very aware of this deep affection between us, often catching us in a quick embrace or sneaking off for a cuddle when we thought nobody was around. They made jokes about it, especially when they got into their teens and, instead of being embarrassed by their parents' unusually passionate relationship, I think they quite liked it. It was better than having parents who had a cold relationship.

During the years I was filming the gardening show with the ABC, my best times were working and socialising with the on-the-road crews who were predominantly men – field producers, cameramen and sound recordists. As a tight-knit team we worked creatively together during the day then invariably let our hair down in the evening over dinner, which would often lead to a night on the town at a disco or karaoke bar. Once again I fell into my old pattern of being one of the boys, kicking up my heels and being a bit outrageous because we were often on location away from our homes and family responsibilities. David never worried about my exploits on the road with the film crews because there simply wasn't anything to worry about. Just Mary and the boys behaving badly, as usual!

During my adult life I have also enjoyed several very close but platonic relationships with older men. I often wondered if these men were substitute father figures because my relationship with my own father had been so troubled and sad. Even David, who is eleven years older than me, could have been categorised as an 'older man' during those early years. I was twenty-one when we first got together; he was a mature thirty-two and had already been through a ten-year marriage that ended not long before I met him. The age difference in the early stage of our relation-ship was more pronounced than it seems today and I can look back and acknowledge that I was seeking the emotional and financial security that I hoped an older man could offer, in contrast to my unstable background.

My most significant relationship with an older man was with a beguiling, witty and well read Irishman called Paddy O'Shaughnessy who lived two houses down the street from our home in Leura and who became part of our family for nearly seventeen years. Paddy had two adult children from his first marriage and then fathered a son with his second wife Margaret. This young boy, Michael, appeared on his scooter the day we first moved into the house, hoping to find boys of the same age to play with. He virtually lived in our backyard until all the children finished school and left home.

The first time I met Paddy, under the brilliant-pink flowering cherry trees that lined our street, he asked – in his lilting Irish brogue – how I was enjoying living in the mountains.

'I just love it,' I gushed. 'The fresh air, the blue skies, the frosty mornings, it's wonderful.'

'And of course the altitude means we are a little closer to God,' he commented, smiling widely.

I thought I must be living next door to a nutcase or a religious fanatic, but quickly discovered that I couldn't have been further off the mark. Paddy was totally irreligious, having survived a tough education at the hands of the Christian Brothers in rural Ireland. He was the illegitimate son of a teenage girl who had been abandoned to the workhouse by her parents' shame at her pregnancy. Miraculously, his grandfather had fetched Paddy home from the institution, leaving his own daughter there, where she somehow managed to get pregnant again and endure the same pain and loneliness. Paddy was reared by his grand-parents then joined the British Air Force and spent most of the war years stationed in the Middle East before migrating to Australia, where he worked on the Snowy Mountains Scheme, like so many postwar immigrants. He always referred to himself as 'an unqualified success' because he had forged a highly successful career as an electrical engineer, based on skills learned in the air force, but without any formal qualifications. When we first knew him he was semi-retired and had the most casually laid-back attitude to life.

'Today, nothing is of the slightest importance' was his creed. This allowed him to spend many guilt-free hours sitting at our kitchen table, drinking cups of tea and smoking cigarettes, whiling away the hours and days and weeks talking to my mother or playing with the children. In many respects he became the grandfather of the family, and I never tired of his company – he could call in any time of the day or night and was always welcome. It was a very special relationship indeed.

My other close older male friend was the former cabinet

minister, senator and judge Jim McClelland, who lived in the next village to us for the last fifteen years of his life. Jim had the same irreverent sense of humour and fun as Paddy, but also a deep understanding of politics and the human condition that made him a great companion. We spent a lot of time together in his last few years, drinking wine, laughing and solving the problems of the world.

When I turned up on Jock's doorstep in France more than a year ago we fell into a warm and comfortable relationship not dissimilar to those I once shared with Paddy and Jim. If my relationship with my own father had been dismal, at least during my adult life I had enjoyed the richness and intelligence of some very interesting older men.

Gradually, I realise that by taking off to France for long periods of time I am not just running away; I am in fact looking for something. It's not just a carefree holiday jaunt, it's a serious attempt to try to discover who I really am after all these decades of nurturing everyone else and virtually ignoring my own needs. In a bookshop before I left Australia I found a weighty tome on menopause and decided that perhaps it's time I did a little reading and research on the subject. Written by an American woman doctor, the book is full of all sorts of spiritual claptrap that is quite meaningless to me, but between the lines are some simple truths that set off alarm bells in my brain. The feelings that this writer describes in such detail are feelings that are overwhelming me on a daily basis. Her explanation of the changes that occur in mid-life are really very straightforward and seem, to me, like good old-fashioned common sense.

It appears that the female hormones essential for pregnancy, childbirth and motherhood have the effect of keeping women in an almost permanent state of passivity. The intricate balance of female hormones is programmed so that she will naturally and quite gladly take on the role of home-maker and caretaker and keeper of the peace. For most women, household harmony is automatically equated with happiness, and so we go to extra-ordinary lengths to maintain an atmosphere of love and safety, warmth and comfort, within the home.

Much has been written about women who, in times of great deprivation and stress, gladly give up their own meagre food and water rations to their children and go without, even if it means they die. This tendency for self-sacrifice isn't a matter of conscious choice. Women are also conditioned to put the needs of others ahead of their own, and while not all women fall for this concept, I certainly recognise a lot of this behaviour in myself. When female hormones are added to the equation, it's quite a combination. I have always believed that my ability to keep the peace in our family was a direct result of my own turbulent childhood, with it's constant drunken brawls and domestic violence. I was determined that my own children would never experience the pain and fear associated with warring parents and I bent over backwards to ensure that the atmosphere in our home was happy and carefree.

My way of dealing with the irritating aspects of my relation-ships – especially my relationships with David and with my mother – was to make jokes about them. I used humour instead of anger as a coping mechanism. I became very good at inventing strategies for jollying everyone along. There was a lengthy period when Mum and David were not speaking after a row about something so trivial that I can't even recall what it was. The atmosphere at mealtimes was leaden as they both sat in sullen silence, refusing to even look at each other. Eventually, I decided to highlight the stupidity of their behaviour by arranging three or four oversize vases of flowers and foliage from the garden down the centre of the table. David was on one side, my mother on the other. David immediately asked what was going on and I simply said, 'Well, if you're not speaking to each other it's probably better if you can't see each other either.'

They both laughed, of course, and the ice was broken. The flowers were removed and they started talking – awkwardly at first, but by the end of the meal the stalemate had been resolved.

That I should have resorted to such elaborate devices to maintain household harmony now seems ludicrous. The veil of peacekeeping has finally lifted and I am, as a result, simply not the same person I was thirty years ago; not physically, not emotionally and not intellectually.

My reading on the subject of menopause also informs me that women's sexuality and libido can undergo dramatic changes at this stage of life. We start to produce testosterone, which can make us more sexually aggressive and may even lead to a change of sexual preference. I am quite shocked at my own feelings of sexuality during this phase. I expected my sexual desires to fade away. I somehow saw fifty as the cut-off point – I would lose interest in lovemaking and throw my energies in other directions – into the garden or my grandchildren. It's certainly the image of middle-aged women that's promoted in the media, and it's one that I believed to be true. But here I am in France, in the mood for kicking up my heels, looking for a little excitement and feeling totally liberated at having abandoned my responsibilities. Reading the book about menopause has somehow reassured me that I am not abnormal, that thousands of women feel just as I do: restless and filled with yearnings for change and fulfilment.

However, the constant references in the book to marriage breakdown do worry me. The author cites dozens of case histories of women who simply walk away from their long-term relationships when they hit menopause. They strike out on their own and make new lives for themselves, much to the shock and dismay of their families, who don't understand the changes that are taking place. One of the main problems, it seems, is the shift in the needs of men and women after thirty years of marriage, especially if the children have left home. Most men at this stage are approaching retirement and they start to look to their family for love and support; even if they have been out and about pursuing their career for decades, suddenly their sphere of interest contracts and they want to spend more time at home developing relationships that may have been on the back burner for years. At exactly the same moment women are coming out of their shell after decades of home-making and nurturing and starting to look outside the home for excitement and fulfilment. It seems that nature plays a cruel trick on us. Or perhaps it's nature's way of saying that we simply don't belong together as couples 'happily ever after'. Sitting alone in the little French house, sipping rosé and nibbling fine Cantal cheese, I wonder if this is what's happening to me.

Some people are sexually predatory, while others spend their whole life hoping that someone else will make the first move. Waiting for the other person to make a pass is undoubtedly easier because it reduces the risk of rejection, and I know that in my younger days, before getting together with David and having a family, I preferred men to make a move in my direction rather than the other way round. During that period of my life I was quite vulnerable to seduction in the sense that I am the sort of woman who finds it very difficult to say no. Not that I was promiscuous – once again it's related to the way women are conditioned not to make others feel uncomfortable or unhappy by rejecting them. That said, if in the past a man did make an overture and I was not interested I could always find a humorous way of deflecting the situation so that it didn't cause hurt or offence. However, if a man I was genuinely attracted to made a move in my direction I found it almost impossible to resist.

I was fortunate, therefore, that I wasn't a single woman for very long, and lucky too that in the many years of my relationship with David there have been no sexually awkward situations that I couldn't wriggle out of with my dignity intact. Looking back at three decades of sexual monogamy I felt proud that I had never been tempted to stray from my marriage bed even though David has spent so much time away from me and the family and I have enjoyed a career involving lots of contact with bright and inter-esting men.

Outsiders might imagine that working in the media, especially in television, is glamorous and sexy. They are fooling themselves. It's a lot of hard work, and the notion of engaging in torrid love affairs at the end of a long day's filming or a day chained to a computer screen is ridiculous. All those years as a full-time working mother served to remind me of how unsexy real life can be. If you make it to the end of the day without collapsing in an exhausted heap you are doing really well. Love affairs, on top of everything else, aren't worth the energy of a passing thought. Even sex with a long-term partner or husband seems a bit tiring when there are deadlines to meet and expectations to be lived up to.

But back in the little house in France, alone and without my husband or the pressure of work and family responsibilities, sex suddenly takes on a different perspective. Is it those troublesome menopausal hormones reminding me that my sexual attractiveness to men is fading away and that if I don't seize the day I might just as well accept that this part of my life is coming to an end? Or maybe I'm curious about having a sexual relationship with another man after three decades? Whatever, I suddenly start looking at the men within my orbit a little differently, and imagining all sorts of interesting possibilities. By putting such a vast physical distance between myself and my spouse, family and friends I have created a situation where I can easily have a love affair without causing too many problems and complications on the home front. Being alone in a French village provides a certain anonymity. I have met dozens of men, some of whom I find most attractive, and they are all great fun to spend time with. I now realise that my pheremones are in full flight, sending out all sorts of unsubtle messages that could be picked up by anyone who is even vaguely sexually predatory. It's a risky but exciting position to be in.

Now, out of the blue, I am contacted by a man I first met last year on one of my overnight sightseeing trips to Toulouse. He is an academic with excellent English, and is handsome and charming, but married. We started chatting in a café one balmy evening and eventually exchanged email addresses and phone numbers. We have loosely kept in touch since I left France last December and now he's proposing I meet him, alone, in Toulouse for lunch. It's pretty obvious to me that lunch isn't all he has on his mind, and my gut reaction is that I should politely say I'm too busy to meet him. But I don't. I say yes, I would love to see him again.

Looking back on this defining moment I realise that I chose an option fraught with danger. My eyes were wide open and I knew exactly what I was getting into. I was determined that I would not leap into bed with this man at the first opportunity but I realised that I was allowing our relationship to move onto a different level. I was opening the door to an intimacy that could lead to a sexual relationship.

What did I feel during this time? I felt incredibly excited yet daunted by the prospect of what might happen between us. I felt a sharp stab of desire coupled with such mental confusion that for days (weeks, months) afterwards I simply couldn't think straight. He phoned every day, sometimes two or three times a day, as we planned a suitable time to meet. Initially, our conversations skirted around the issues but the more we talked – or, rather, flirted shamelessly on the phone – the more open and honest we were with each other about how we were feeling, about the direction in which our relationship was heading, about the possibility of a dangerous liaison.

For me it was a time of great confusion, and I felt alarmed and unsettled. I felt like a different person – and in many ways I *was* a different person from the one I had been even two or three years ago. The voice that spoke so candidly with this man, responding to sexual innuendo, was not my voice. It was the voice of another woman, an adventurous, free-spirited woman who didn't care about risking her marriage and her family and her new farm. She just cared about the exciting possibilities that lay ahead.

I didn't talk to anyone about what was happening, but I think some of my friends in France sensed that I was rattled and edgy. At dinner parties and lunches and friendly gatherings I talked vaguely around the subject of long-term relationships and infidelity. The topic was obviously weighing heavily on my mind.

Jock summed it up beautifully by telling me as I sat in his sunny courtyard one autumn lunchtime enjoying pastis, 'You know, Mary, it doesn't actually count as adultery if it happens in another country.'

I think he understood where I was coming from.

14

After several weeks of long-distance flirtation and discussion and planning, the proposed trip to Toulouse for a meeting with my potential lover becomes an impossibility because of my work commitments and the fact that he must suddenly go to Paris to attend an urgent meeting. We have run out of time and missed our opportunity. I feel a sense of relief mixed with a profound feeling of disappointment. We stay in constant communication and discuss the possibility of getting together when I return to France next year. It seems a long time to wait, but it will add a certain edge to the relationship, an anticipation and yearning that will make the meeting even more exciting. It will also give me much needed time to think about it and analyse what's going on here. After all, we are both married and past the age where casual sex or one-night stands are likely to be really satisfying. We are walking down the path towards a much deeper involvement and, in every respect, an emotional relationship is far more dangerous to a marriage than a sudden, impulsive sexual encounter.

Instead of my usual cheerful, chatty self I am on edge and feeling so frail and unsettled that David detects a change in my voice when we talk on the phone. He says I sound 'disturbed' and asks if I am okay. Initially, I reassure him that everything's fine, that I'm just tired from too much socialising. But he persists in questioning me and eventually I tell him a little about the phone conversations I've have been having with the man from Toulouse, whom he has never met. He becomes very quiet, almost withdrawn, and simply tells me to take care and not exhaust myself. I realise that after living with me for so many years, David can probably read me like a book. It's not really surprising that he senses a change in me simply from my tone of voice. He's obviously worried but not likely to make a big fuss about a few phone calls, even if they are with another man. Yet I am also aware that this is what he has been fearing for some time, since I first 'ran away' last year to live alone. Back then we discussed the possibility that I was planning to have a fling while in France. He made several half-joking references to it and I simply laughed them off. Although at the same time I teasingly taunted him with jokes about French lovers, I didn't seriously think it was on the cards. I wasn't feeling confident enough about my own appearance or attractiveness to imagine that I would be in a position to engage in illicit relationships during my travels. How wrong I was.

It's just a few days before I am due to fly back to Australia and I fill them by saying farewell over lunches and dinners with my friends, taking long walks in and around the village, playing music (probably too loudly) and drinking wine (probably too much). I am overwhelmed by a sense of melancholia. What am I doing with my life? Here I am hurtling headlong into an emotional relationship with a man I don't really know very well, betraying the trust of my already long-suffering husband and threatening to wreak havoc in all directions. The alarming reality of it all, from my perspective, is that the more I talk with the man, the more smitten I am by him. He's bright, charming and very funny, and there's nothing sexier than a man who can make you laugh. I realise that a certain mechanism is kicking in here: I am actually falling in love with this man, possibly because it's the only way I will allow myself to become sexually involved with him. Like a lot of women, I am probably not capable of satisfying sex without a deeper involvement, and now I have months and months where our relationship can only develop via phone and email. It's a worrying and quite daunting prospect.

On my return to Australia at the end of October, I am immediately launched into the release of the book I finished writing earlier in the year. We have decided to use French words in the title – *Au Revoir* (which translates more accurately as 'farewell until we see each other again' rather than just 'goodbye') – with the added teaser line 'Running Away from Home at Fifty', which I believe will appeal to plenty of women of my generation. I am confronted by the usual barrage of media interviews that surround a book launch, including print and television but mostly radio. One of the first interviews is with Geraldine Doogue on her Radio National morning program 'Life Matters'. Geraldine read the book just before publication and wants to be first cab off the rank with an interview. Logistically we have problems finding a time to suit us both, as Geraldine prefers a face-to-face interview rather than one over the phone. In the end we compromise, with me in a booth at the ABC studios in Orange and Geraldine in Sydney. With this type of technology it still sounds like an intimate interview, not a prerecorded or telephone talk.

Before the interview starts we have a chance for a brief chat and Geraldine tells me how much she has enjoyed the book, how brave she thinks I am to have written it in such a candid fashion. I've never really thought about it being brave – just honest, really. If you are writing down the memories of your life there's really no alternative but to be totally honest.

The interview is gruelling. I suppose I imagine that we will chat a bit about my past but probably concentrate on what I consider to be the main thrust of the book – the desire of a woman in middle age to strike out and do something for herself rather than continue with an overcrowded life. But no, Geraldine is far more intrigued by the family story – the drinking and fighting, the suicides, the disappearance of my sister Margaret, the death of my baby sister Jane and the pain of growing up in such a disordered environment – all the material I initially resisted writing about but expanded on when prompted by my publisher. I answer every question as openly and honestly and with as much good humour as possible. Listening to it played back afterwards, I certainly sound as though I am enjoying the interview, just like a lively and intimate conversation. This, of course, is exactly how it is meant to sound. But inside I begin to feel a sense of panic, that I have revealed too much and opened myself up for close scrutiny by strangers. I bounce out of the studio into David's arms – he has been listening to every word in the soundproof radio booth next door.

'That was a fantastic interview,' he says 'very powerful and involving.'

'Let's get out of here, quickly,' I reply, barely able to hold back my tears.

In the car I sob for thirty minutes. I am shaken and dismayed. It was incredibly naive of me, a trained journalist, not to realise the implications of what I had written in *Au Revoir*. What had I expected? You cannot chronicle such a vivid and disturbing story without expecting some reaction from those who read it. I suppose I believed that because I had written my family story in an accepting and almost cheerful fashion, the elemental truths of it would not upset or disturb those who read it – another naive assumption. And I suppose I believed that having processed the trauma by writing it down, I would now be immune to being upset by it.

I do what members of my family always do in crisis – I drag David to the Orange RSL Club for a stiff drink, even though it's only 11.30 in the morning.

Gradually, the realisation that I have written something a little more confronting and thought-provoking than *A Year in Provence* settles in. I continue on the publicity merry-go-round and the book leaps off the shelves in the lead-up to Christmas. It is reprinted several times over the next six months and I am inundated with cards and letters from readers who identify with it in many and various ways.

'I felt like a sister-in-spirit with you, through sharing your delights and fears in all matters of life,' says one letter.

'As a boomer myself, I felt I could come into your kitchen and have a cuppa and a good chat.'

'Reading your accounts of the viciousness and violence between your parents helped me to understand how this came to be played out in my own life.'

'I've been moved – in fact quite emotional – reading your adventures, but more importantly your reflections in *Au Revoir*.

Your mother–daughter insights are significant for me.'

'I have to say how much I related to you at different times in the book but especially your reason for trying it.'

'I would like to tell you how happy I felt for you having taken the huge step of leaving home and travelling and living alone.'

It is a surprise to get all these positive, warm and funny letters from people, such a change from all those years of writing gardening books, where the mail consisted of little more than 'I tried your recipe for garlic spray and it worked wonderfully on my cabbages!'

The afternoon that the Geraldine Doogue interview goes to air, I receive a phone call from her office. In an excited voice, one of the producers tells me that when the segment was played on radio in Perth (three hours behind Sydney because of the time zones) they had a call from a woman who not only knew my sister Margaret but had kept in touch with her all these years.

The effect of this news on me is totally overwhelming. My daughter Miriam and David are both in the room at the time I take the phone call and they can testify to my reaction. It's a physical reaction. As I hang up the phone I collapse onto my desk and find it difficult to breathe, let alone speak. It's hours before I am composed enough to pick up the phone and call Perth. A warm, mature woman answers.

'Margaret and I taught together and travelled together to Canada in the 1960s. She's still there, living on Vancouver Island with her husband Ken,' she tells me.

David and Miriam are concerned at the intensity of my reaction. While they both know that I have been wanting to find my sister for many years, I don't think they understand just how emotional I feel about her. It's been a very private sadness for me, and like everything in my life that causes me pain I have locked it away somewhere so that I don't have to experience it. Now it's out there and I have to confront all my fears about making contact with Margaret: the possibility of rejection and the overwhelming thought that I might finally get to meet her, face to face.

After a restless night with little sleep I write to Margaret and send, via express courier, a copy of *Au Revoir*. It's an easy letter to write, almost as though I've been rehearsing the words all my adult life.

This is a letter I have yearned to write for many years, but never knew where I could send it until today. I have a book, just published, which I have enclosed. This morning I did a national radio interview, talking about the book, and it led to my finally discovering an address for you after all these years. One of your old teaching friends phoned the radio station.

The book, when you read it, will explain just about everything there is to know about what has happened over the past fifty years. It skims the surface, of course, but it will certainly fill you in on some of the detail. I never really intended the book to be about our family – it started off as a sort of travelogue, a diary of the six months I spent in France last year. But somehow a lot of the old stories came tumbling out when I sat down to write.

I sincerely hope that you will not find this sudden connection with the past too painful. Nothing would give me greater pleasure than to see you again. Without being overly sentimental, I have always felt as though part of my life was missing. It would be just so wonderful to talk and maybe even laugh about some of the things of the past.

As I post the envelope in Bathurst I start to worry about Margaret's reaction to hearing from me after all these years. I assume that she made a new life for herself because of the extreme difficulties of her childhood, probably similar to the ones I experienced in the same household. I visualise her getting the package and seeing my name on the back and wondering what on earth it is all about. The days after sending the book are long and anxious.

To my great relief, within ten days a card arrives from Canada, from Margaret. I have been rushing down the long drive to the front gate every morning and suddenly here it is. I tear the envelope in my eagerness to open it and read the contents.

Dear Mary,

I was truly pleased to hear from you. Your package arrived early on a particularly busy day and I was just unable to get to it until the evening. My first inclination was to go straight to your book.

However, I only managed to get through about forty pages before I found myself overwhelmed. You write beautifully but clearly. The images and memories revived were just too much for me. Please allow me to slow down the pace and I will respond to you fully when I have managed to cope with my visit to my other life.

Love Margaret.

I have a sister. She has written to me and she will write to me again. I can't remember ever feeling so elated. At last the piece of the jigsaw puzzle missing in my life has been found.

16

Living on a farm in Australia, even a small farm such as ours, is a responsibility. Land ownership isn't just a right afforded to those with the resources to purchase acreage. It involves caring for the entire environment, not just the postage stamp of land that you own but all the land that surrounds it and the waterways that run through it, if you are fortunate enough to acquire land with water.

Our farm is perfect for us in many ways. It doesn't involve us in being responsible for large areas of land – only ten hectares – and it has good water resources in the form of a deep spring, a good-sized dam also fed from a spring and a small stream running along the front of the property with the typically rural name of Frying Pan Creek. It is also located on the Sydney side of Bathurst, which makes journeys to the city easier and faster.

The house was built by Bill and Mabel Walshaw sometime between 1910 and 1915 and is a curious mixture of styles. The main shape of the building and verandahs is Federation but the five tall chimney pots look more Victorian and, inside, the fireplace surrounds are a mixture of Art Nouveau and classic colonial. It's constructed from the deep red slender bricks characteristic of the Bathurst region and the roof is tin and still original, though badly in need of restoration when we bought it. Originally known as Ickleton, the house was quite grand for the region, with deep verandahs on three sides and a maid's quarters at the rear of the house behind the laundry. There is a servery area from the large walk-in pantry to the formal dining room, and all the ceilings are ornate patterned plaster and in perfect condition. The interior woodwork – doors, skirting boards and architraves – are of cedar and have thankfully never been painted. Instead, they were coated with a dark shellac which can be stripped back, although I doubt we will ever have the energy or time to do so. There are five bedrooms, including a large main bedroom with a small but highly efficient open fireplace, indicative of the sort of weather experienced here in the winter. There are two elaborate interior fireplaces in the formal living and dining rooms, and a wood-burning stove for cooking in the kitchen. That one also heats the water, so is in use most days of the year.

The Walshaw family had been established here at Yetholme for many decades – they are listed in the 1872 postal directory – but Bill Walshaw left to seek his fortune on the goldfields of Western Australia early in the twentieth century and stayed away for some years before returning with his wife Mabel to build Ickleton, which was described, in its day, as a 'substantial residence'. Bill and Mabel must have done quite well from their goldmining adventures because the house is constructed of good-quality materials and would cost a small fortune to build now in the same quality and style. They didn't have children of their own but raised Mabel Walshaw's nephew and two nieces, brought back with them from the goldfields. The children's father was the mine manager at Meekatharra and their mother had died, so they were taken in and educated by their kindly aunt and uncle.

The Walshaws were quite prominent in the district, and in the 1930s they built a community hall at the rear of the house. The hall which served as an entertainment centre and meeting place for the locals. It still stands today, in excellent condition, and has been used for a variety of community purposes, including the local ballet school, for decades. In Bathurst itself the Walshaws also contributed financially to many good causes, including a handsome church hall for the local Anglican community.

In 1972 Ickleton was bought by a local charitable organisation, Glenray Industries, which provided residential accommodation and sheltered workshops for local people with intellectual disabilities. During this period the name was changed to Glenray Park and the house was transformed into an institution with the bedrooms set up as dormitories and three glassed-in sleepouts on the verandahs. One of the bedrooms was converted into a toilet block with bath, shower and two toilets. The living room was in fact one of the smallest bedrooms, while the small formal sitting room had been made into a dormitory. To my knowledge there were sixteen to twenty residents and two full-time staff, which means the place must have been bursting at the seams, although people who remember it say it always seemed roomy and comfortable. An old houseparents' record book was left behind and it makes fascinating reading, with tales of blocked toilets and water pumps breaking down and residents being 'grounded for behaving badly when in town'. All this took place in the days before institutions were closed down to make way for group houses so that people with disabilities could live 'out in the community', and it seems as though it was a model of good management. Some of the locals who worked out here recall that it had a family atmosphere and that the residents were totally accepted into the community and included in all the local dances, concerts and fairs.

Under supervision, the Glenray Park residents ran the small property as a farm – it had an extensive orchard, a huge vegetable garden, milking cows and sheep. The residents worked not just to provide for their own needs but also to have produce to sell, and some of this income went directly into their own pockets.

In the mid-1990s Glenray Park closed down and the residents moved into Bathurst. It was purchased by a young couple who converted it back into a residential home, stripping out the toilet block and tearing down some of the sleepouts.

The old house was in good condition when we bought it, although at the time it seemed rather crazy for David and me with none of our children still living at home to be rattling around in a five-bedroomed house. Quickly, however, the bedrooms have filled as our children come with their children for weekend visits. The community hall has easily transformed into a spacious playroom for all the kids, doubling as a terrific place for large family parties when the weather is less than perfect.

The weather is challenging in this neck of the woods. It's one of the coldest little pockets of the state, sitting at an altitude of 1200 metres, and with a winter climate similar to Oberon –

hovering between minus five and eight degrees on average. When the Great Western Highway is closed by ice or snow, it's usually on the stretch of road two minutes from our front door. The frosts are frightening, sometimes freezing the walnut flowers right off the trees. The first winter we were there, they completely destroyed the spring display on a 100 year-old wisteria. The ground freezes and gardening is out of the question except in the middle of the day.

17

My first real period of living on the farm comes after I return from France in late October, following the flurry of activity surrounding the release of *Au Revoir*. We had sold the house in Leura without too much trouble and during the period before settlement had gradually started moving our possessions out to the farm, storing them in one of the sheds. The main move, which took three days to complete, had occured just days before I left for France, so when I return it is to a reasonable amount of chaos. There are dozens of boxes to unpack, bookshelves to build and paintings to hang. My problem is that I simply don't have the heart for it. Normally I am a person who charges at work at a thousand miles an hour. Although I've only moved house twice in thirty years, both times I had the house settled and arranged within days – floors polished, rugs scattered and a vase of flowers on every table. This time I wander aimlessly from room to room, back and forth from the shed where all our office equipment and files are stored, simply looking at what needs to be done and feeling totally daunted. My heart is in France and I am feeling so confused and confronted by my feelings for the man in Toulouse that everything here on the farm seems trivial. How could my entire attitude to life change in four short weeks? Instead of embracing this old house as our family home, I look around and wonder what I am doing here. It all seems so pointless.

David immediately senses my unsettled mood. Although he hasn't said much about our strained conversations when I was still in France, he is well aware that I am in a strange frame of mind. I try denying that anything is amiss. I try to blame my fluctuating hormones for the fact that I have become withdrawn and, at times, deeply melancholic. But he knows there is more to it than that and keeps probing until eventually I tell him how I am feeling, about my confusion and yearning for the man from Toulouse.

His reaction is, understandably, quite intense.

Once I manage to reassure him that the relationship has not actually been consummated, he starts to put forward a strong case for my ending the liaison there and then. Initially I resist, saying that I believe it is important for the relationship to 'run its course'. I argue that because I have been with him since I was only twenty-one years old, I have a right to other sexual experiences and that it is only natural that after thirty-one years I should feel a need to explore my sexuality outside our marriage. I debate various long-term issues in our relationship: his absence over the years, his emotional and sexual unavailability, his ongoing moodiness and depression. I make it clear that I am no longer prepared to tolerate aspects of our relationship that I have been tolerating for decades.

The arguments simply don't wash. David's reaction to the

possibility of my entering into an emotional and loving relationship with another man is totally negative and passionately intense. But suddenly something else is happening between us. While we are raging and at times screaming at each other we realise that we are communicating on a level that we haven't reached for years. There is a new openness, honesty and intimacy that has evaded us till now. It is painful but exciting to feel the dynamics of our relationship shifting and changing with such power. More than this, the intensity of our sexual relationship also changes dramatically. From several years of complacency, David is shaken into a realisation that I am no longer satisfied with the occasional, almost routine, lovemaking. He has reached that crucial age for men – 60 plus – when sexual function is no longer automatic, and he has been taking the easy option of allowing our relationship on that level to dwindle. The possibility of losing me to another man acts as a powerful aphrodisiac and suddenly we are making love as we haven't done for years. It is energising and exciting but it adds greatly to my confusion. In France I had felt justified in contemplating an adulterous relationship because of a lack of intimacy with my husband. Now I don't have any real justification.

During the following months, when I am feeling unhappy and unsettled, David is supportive and loving. Having suffered depression on and off he knows how debilitating it can be, how hard it is to feel motived on days when life seems quite pointless and even the simplest of routine tasks seem too difficult. He's never really seen me in this state of mind so he worries a lot, but is always there for me. It helps me feel that I am not entirely alone. I discuss the situation with Miriam as well and tell her about the relationship that has been developing in France. She is compassionate because she appreciates how difficult I have found life with her father over the decades, but she is also highly protective of our family unit and urges me to put the thought of a love affair to one side and try instead to heal my relationship with David.

Meanwhile, I am in almost daily contact with my Toulouse man, either by email or by calls that are set up by email. I let him know when David is not at home and he calls me – often on his mobile phone because he, too, needs to be out of his home when he makes contact. The intensity of our long-distance foreplay doesn't subside and I indicate to him that I am having problems at home and that my husband is aware that I am involved with another man.

'You must tell him nothing,' he insists. 'It will be very bad for your relationship with him. He must not know, not now, not ever.'

So I go underground. Or at least I think I do.

I tell David that I have terminated my relationship with my proposed lover, that it is completely over and that he is to stop worrying. I know that I am not a very good liar, but I do my best to reassure David that everything is now fine and back on an even keel.

He isn't, as it turns out, fooled for a moment.

I try my best to lift my spirits out of the trough, but somehow I am living in a completely unreal state of mind. I am desperately trying to love being on the farm, to love my husband and continue being a good wife, loving mother and involved grandmother. But in my heart I am in another place, another space, another time. My thoughts are constantly straying into the realms of my fantasy love affair. I simply can't get it out of my mind. I lose weight, dramatically. I can't sleep – or at least I go to sleep initially then wake up at 3 am and lie awake for the rest of the night, tossing and turning in troubled thought. I finally doze off at 6.30 am, waking up shortly afterwards consumed by a feeling of sadness that I can't explain. Waking up sad – it has never happened to me in my life, not even during those troubled childhood years when I was surrounded by the insecurity of domestic violence and family chaos. I catch David looking at me, concerned, asking if I am feeling okay.

'You look so sad,' he says. 'What's wrong?'

'Nothing,' I say, attempting cheerfulness. 'Nothing.'

But he knows.

When David and I make love I don't fantasise that he is the man from Toulouse, and for this I am relieved. However, just about every other waking moment is spent visualising and fantasising about the moment when I will eventually meet him. Lying in bed in the middle of the night, with David sleeping soundly beside me, I play out the drama and romance of that moment in my head. Sometimes we meet on a railway platform, sometimes in a restaurant, sometimes in the street. Although I don't know him very well I have developed a strong visual image of him in my mind and I also have a clear sense of his character from our ongoing illicit conversations. He's very straight up and down and direct and, even though our relationship is based on deception, between us there is an honesty that I find reassuring. There's no game playing here. We discuss the nature of our attraction for each other and the implications of our future liaison, and we both agree that the feelings between us are strong enough to be disturbing. He seems to be as rattled by the whole thing as I am.

I clearly remember the sensation of falling in love for the first time as a teenager. It was like a sickness that overwhelmed my body and mind, manifesting in physical symptoms like nausea and heart palpitations. I lost the ability to concentrate and my head was constantly filled with thoughts of my new love. More than thirty years later I'm experiencing the same feelings, and while I find it exhilarating, it is also causing me a great deal of pain and anxiety. I don't wish to hurt David, but I know that for my own sake I need to see this relationship through, to reach a conclusion.

Part of my feeling so odd during this period is the realisation that I am thinking and behaving abnormally. Lifelong habits have disappeared and been replaced by quite different patterns of behaviour. All my life I have been a dedicated fan of classical music, with a large collection of Beethoven, Mozart, Rachmaninov and Vivaldi. Now I am buying and playing albums of soppy love songs by Eva Cassidy and Luka Bloom, and listening to favourites from my teenage years – Donovan, Cat Stevens, Simon and Garfunkel and Bob Dylan. All my adult life I have read a daily newspaper cover to cover, but now I can't be bothered. I don't have the concentration for novels either. I have always managed to read a book every week. Now I haven't opened one for months. I stare at the ceiling instead and daydream. Instead of looking outwards and embracing the world, my thoughts are all self-directed.

Feeling for the first time, ever, that I am out of control, I decide that the onset of menopause is connected to my extreme lack of energy and enthusiasm for life here at the farm. Disconcerted at my inability to cope with even the most prosaic of domestic problems or challenges, I consult various doctors, start a regime of hormones and, at the prompting of a friend, begin seeing a counsellor once a week to talk through my feelings.

My friend is concerned that my mid-life unhappiness may well be connected to the traumas of my childhood and that they are only now beginning to surface as a result of the hormone change experienced in menopause.

In my wildest dreams I have never imagined that I would be a candidate for this type of help and I've often made insensitive jokes about the proliferation of counsellors in modern society. It has seemed to me that every trivial trauma in life these days necessitates professional intervention, and that it has become a growth industry. I have believed, quite arrogantly, that nothing can replace family support as the most natural form of coun-selling, yet here I am surrounded by a large and loving family, none of whom can help me out of my misery.

It is unnerving to sit and talk about myself for hours at a time, almost as unnerving as writing about myself and my family in *Au Revoir*. At the gentle prompting of my counsellor I start with my childhood and talk my way through my life. She listens with an open mind to the story of my ups and downs. In many ways it's an unremarkable story, because so many people survive much more difficult childhoods and develop all sorts of strategies for coping with life's problems. The counsellor asks lots of questions and throws many of the issues I raise back at me, forcing me to question my interpretation of aspects of and incidents in my life and the ways in which I handle them. At no point does she offer me advice or tell me what to do. She simply draws me out of my shell and allows me, by talking candidly, to draw my own conclusions.

What I begin to understand for myself as a result of these counselling sessions is that I do indeed carry a deep well of dis-satisfaction about my relationship with David, that I resent his constant absences over so many years and his emotional distance from me and our children. Looking back over the years, I believe that his passion has all been directed towards his work. Yet I know that he has always loved me deeply and adores his children and now his grandchildren. It's just that in several ways he hasn't been there for us.

The counselling sessions also help me look at myself more objectively and to realise that my self-esteem is low. In spite of my career achievements and the fact that I have also enjoyed success as a parent and home-maker, I feel very insecure about my own abilities and worth. This is not an unusual way for a survivor of a troubled family to behave.

'You have a very ready smile,' my counsellor says. 'An instant smile that's very attractive. It gives the impression of openness and happiness. But often people who smile a lot do so because it's a mask. Often a wide smile is used to hide an inner unhappiness or nervousness or insecurity,' she adds.

Little bells of recognition start ringing all around my brain.

18

Many of the girls I went to school with in the 1960s were much more sexually precocious and liberated than I was. Much of it was due to their advanced physical maturity, as most of them had visibly curvaceous bodies at thirteen or fourteen when I was still flat-chested and without a single strand of pubic hair. Females reach the menarche earlier and earlier with each subsequent generation, and these days it's not uncommon for girls of ten or eleven to start menstruation and to have to cope with all the associated physical and emotional changes that this hormonal state brings. I was sixteen before I had my first period – years behind my girlfriends, many of whom were already sexually active and taking the pill. In many ways I was glad to be a late starter because it afforded me a certain sense of innocence and safety. While my girlfriends had boys phoning them for dates and were pleading with their mothers to be allowed out on Saturday night, I was still happy to stay at home and watch television with the family cat on my lap.

I sometimes stayed overnight at the homes of my girlfriends, and when they giggled and talked furtively about their experiences with boys it was over my head. I remember staying with one friend, sleeping top to toe in her narrow single bed, when we were woken at 2 am by a vigorous knock on the window glass. She opened the window and there was a burly young man in his early twenties, smelling strongly of beer. She clambered out in her cotton shortie pyjamas and disappeared for what seemed like an eternity. It was probably just half an hour. I lay there, wondering what on earth was going on. Later, when she climbed back and snuggled into bed, I asked her.

'Who was that? What were you doing?'

'Don't be such an idiot, Mary,' she said and promptly dropped back to sleep.

It was months before the penny dropped. One of my other friends told me she was in love with one of the boys in the local football team and that they were 'doing it'.

I was shocked.

Eventually I started going out with boys, but I was seldom invited out by anyone that I really fancied. Several boys attempted to grope me while kissing – in the back seat of a car or the back row of a cinema – but I was so afraid that their hands would find their way to my empty bra that I fended them off. I thus retained my virginity long after everyone else had cheerfully surrendered theirs to the passion of youth.

One girlfriend decided I needed some lessons in the art of romance and lovemaking. Staying at her house one night while her parents were out, she determined that I would benefit greatly from kissing lessons and we spent several hours rolling around on the sofa locked in a sticky embrace. I remember how soft and smooth the skin of her face felt and how nice it must be for men, with their rough, bristly chins, to kiss women for that very reason.

When I finally did lose my virginity it was not by choice; it was because I was raped. I was at a party at the home of a boy whose family I had never met and, as was usual at these gatherings, the parents were out for the evening. I had gone with a boy who had asked me out several times before but who had never even attempted to hold my hand, let alone put his hand up my blouse. He owned a car, which was a major advantage, and it was a strange but quite comfortable arrangement from my point of view.

Like a lot of Australian parties, it split into two groups. The boys gathered in one corner to discuss sport or beer or cars while the girls floated around in smaller groups, not talking much at all but listening to music and sometimes dancing. I had drunk several beers when a young man, quite short and with a stocky build, came over and started chatting to me. I had never seen him before – in fact, he seemed to appear from nowhere – and he was charming. It was really nice to have an animated conversation with a boy, especially as he wasn't trying to flirt with me or use any of the pick-up lines that girls expect at parties where everyone is drinking.

After half an hour he suddenly said to me, 'Come out here for a moment, I've got something to show you.'

'What?' I asked. 'What do you want me to see?'

'It's a surprise,' he said. 'Come on,', and he took me by the hand.

Because he was so bright and pleasant and hadn't attempted to make a pass at me, it didn't occur to me that there was anything sinister in those words. We walked onto the verandah and down some steps into the garden, where it was quite dark.

'Where on earth are you taking me?' I asked, still not feeling even vaguely uneasy.

He laughed. 'Just wait a moment, you'll see,' he said.

We walked down the side lane of the house and suddenly he pushed me very hard into a timber door that burst open. The room was pitch black and I realised it was the laundry under the house. He slammed the door shut, grabbed me with one hand and put his other hand hard over my mouth.

'Shut up, you stupid bitch. Don't you dare scream,' he hissed.

I must have been in total shock. I don't remember fighting hard, but I certainly struggled a lot and started to cry. He was incredibly strong and insistent and somehow managed to tear my clothes off, throwing them into what I realised later was a laundry tub full of water. As he pushed me down onto the concrete floor I really started to fight back.

I told him I was a virgin and he laughed nastily, forcing his hand over my mouth again while pushing my legs apart. 'Don't be ridiculous, of course you're not,' he said. Then he pushed himself against me.

He quickly realised that I must have been telling the truth as penetrating me was much more difficult than he expected. He started to get angry with my struggling and by this time he was also really abusive. I was genuinely frightened and decided to stop fighting. In a matter of minutes it was done. He quickly readjusted his clothing and was gone, vanished into the night.

I found a light switch and retrieved my soaking clothes from the laundry tub. I was badly shaken and my back was bleeding from being scraped along the concrete floor. I was, of course, also bleeding from between my legs.

God knows how I must have looked when I went back, bedraggled and bleeding, to the party. Everyone gathered round as I told them what had happened. Nobody remembered having even seen the young man in question and certainly nobody laid claim to knowing him. A couple of the boys ran up and down the street looking for him, but there was no trace. There was no suggestion that the police be called, or that any further action be taken.

The boy who had taken me to the party was strangely quiet and withdrawn. 'I'd better take you home,' he said. Not a word passed between us on that journey and he never telephoned me or asked me out again. I guess he thought, somehow, it was my fault. I never told my parents or any of my schoolfriends and it was years and years before I ever spoke about it to anyone.

When I did, however, I handled it as a humorous anecdote, more or less the same way I've always handled the painful aspects of my life. I made a joke of losing my virginity on a cold, hard laundry floor in the middle of winter, and of having to climb back into wet clothing and face a room full of amazed people. Just another funny story in which I conveniently left out the pain, humiliation and fear.

Remarkably, having survived such a brutal introduction to sex, I went on to form a couple of very happy and satisfying long-term sexual relationships, one of which has lasted. I often wondered if the young man in question did this sort of thing regularly – crashed parties to which he hadn't been invited and targeted vulnerable girls. Or if it was just a one-off situation and I was simply stupid and naive. It didn't shatter my confidence or make me nervous around men, but it certainly taught me a valuable if painful lesson about how easy it is for a woman to get into a situation in which she has very little control. I look back now and wonder whether I could have screamed or possibly kicked harder or fought back more vigorously. But we were a long way from the party, behind heavy brick walls, with loud music blaring and I had little chance of being rescued.

My first long-term relationship was with one of the boys from my gang, a bright and lovable young man who had been expelled from several schools, including a prestigious private boarding school, for rebellious behaviour. His name was also David, and he was clever in every sense and also highly talented artistically. He was tall, almost six foot six, with a tangle of long black hair and arresting aquiline features. He looked like a cross between Tiny Tim and Frank Zappa, only to my eyes much handsomer than either of them.

David was a problem for his parents. He lacked motivation to study and dropped out of school, despite the fact that for most of his school life he had been a top student. He also totally lacked motivation to work and spent most of his days in bed, reading, sleeping or watching television, and most of his nights partying – drinking, talking to friends and smoking dope. I adored him.

What attracted me to men, I realise now, from my middle-aged perspective, was a desperate need in me to be needed. David needed me because, like most eighteen-year-old boys, he needed sex. By this time I was mature enough and had put my earlier trauma behind me so I was a willing, more than willing, partner. David also needed me because when I left school I immediately got a job and had an income. I was his passport to freedom in the sense that I could pay the rent in a share house and make it possible for him to live away from home. I was also a 'doer'. I was willing to do the shopping, the cooking and the cleaning as well as pay the bills then jump into bed as fresh as a daisy. I must have been mad, and although I knew deep down that the relationship was doomed from the start, I was so blinded by first love that I didn't care. My parents were horrified at my choice of boyfriend, although they were so engrossed in their own problems that they didn't create much of a fuss when I left home to live with him. My girlfriends from school thought he was a 'weirdo' because of the way he looked and dressed. Most of them were attracted to football players or university students with short hair and fast cars.

David spent a lot of his time being sad and depressed and I spent a lot of my time trying to make him feel happy and loved. He was a very gentle and sweet person, but the relationship was totally out of balance in terms of 'give' and 'take'. In spite of this we remained together for three years until he took off to London using an airline ticket given to him by his parents for his twenty-first birthday. I was shattered when he left without me, but resolved to save furiously and join him as quickly as I could. I took a second job, as a barmaid working nights in the Mosman Hotel, but my attempts at amassing enough money for my own airfare to the UK were constantly thwarted because he kept phoning me in desperation. He had failed to get a job (if truth be known, he had failed to look for a job) and was constantly running out of money. So every few weeks I would post off my meagre savings to prevent him from starving to death (or running out of funds for dope).

As I said, I was stupid.

Then I met David number two and my life took a turn for the better. A much older man, David not only had a job and a car and been married before but had recently separated from his girlfriend and was feeling very sorry for himself. I was just the tonic he needed, so once again I had stumbled upon a man who needed me. He loved to eat. I loved to cook. He tended to a negative perspective on life. I had a more positive and optimistic view of the world. We were a good balance and, best of all, he wanted to look after me. Since we started living together within days of first going out, it's remarkable that our relationship has lasted as long as it has.

During those early years together we didn't even contemplate marriage, mainly because David hadn't gone through the motions of getting divorced from his first wife. We had our three children out of wedlock and this never worried me for one moment. I was completely laid-back about the status of a formal or legal 'marriage' as the foundation of a relationship. We were 'a couple,' as married and committed as any two people who had walked down the aisle or paid a visit to the registry office. In those days the term 'partner' had not been coined, and I used to find it amusing to think of ways to describe David when I introduced him to people, especially in more conservative situations such as school speech nights or fundraisers. I often opted for 'my fiancé', which I delivered with a wry smile. David seemed to have no trouble introducing me as his 'wife' but I was almost defiantly proud of our living-in-sin status. I suppose it was just part of the inner rebelliousness engendered by my unconventional upbringing.

We were always totally open with our children about the fact that we were not officially married. I made jokes about it and treated the whole subject lightly. Our youngest son Ethan, when about seven years of age, curtly corrected his primary school teacher, who was giving them a lesson on names, explaining how women generally changed their surnames, to that of their husband after marriage.

'Sometimes, however, professional women keep their maiden name because that is what they are known by,' the teacher innocently told the class. 'For example,' he continued, 'Ethan Hannay's mother is a journalist and she is still known by her maiden name of Mary Moody.'

'That's wrong, Sir,' Ethan immediately chimed in. 'The reason my mother still uses her maiden name is because my parents aren't married.'

When he recounted this exchange to me after school, I didn't know whether to be amused or concerned. On the one hand I was pleased that he was so forthright and truthful; on the other, I wondered what discussion took place in the staffroom that afternoon. At the end of the day, it didn't really matter.

Eventually David did get a divorce from his first wife and we decided to get married although, looking back, I can't understand why we felt the need to formalise our living situation. I was very keen that people didn't think our wedding was going to be sentimental or romantic, but somehow it turned out to be both, as friends from two decades gathered with our teenage children and members of both our families to celebrate our past, present and future. I kept saying that it was just an excuse to have a terrific party – which it was – but there must have been a greater need for the security that a wedding certificate provides.

It never occurred to me that my marriage could founder at a later stage, although lots of our friends said jokingly that getting married after so many years of living together was a sure-fire way of breaking up a good relationship. We laughed.

I have always been very positive and good-humoured, and hell-bent on having fun, no matter what the situation. It's my Irish roots. David is a Scot, through and through, tending to be serious, taking a more negative approach and often slipping into dark periods of depression. Yet if you had asked our children – at any stage of their growing up – they would have said that our marriage was as solid as a rock. Our friends would have said the same thing – not that anyone on the outside can really know or understand the truth about a friend's marriage. But David and I had a comfortable, trusting and loving partnership with the odd fireworks thrown in just to keep life interesting.

Everything, I realise, has shifted. Now, with the possibility of another relationship simmering in the background, I find it increasingly difficult to tolerate certain aspects of my day-to-day life with David. Things that I have been turning a blind eye to for decades are now driving me totally demented. The fact that he is at home every day and is relishing the fact that we have so much time to spend in each other's company only adds to my irritation. Although he still has an office in Sydney, he rarely goes there unless it's for important meetings, and then he usually does it in one day, driving down early in the morning and getting home just in time for dinner. His joy at our being together, alone, for so much of the time drives me into an even greater tangle of fury and frustration.

'It's all very well for you to be here now, doing the washing and the shopping and feeding the bloody chickens,' I rail. 'But where were you when I really needed you, when the children were growing up, when they were teenagers and being difficult?'

He shakes his head and looks deeply hurt. Where is the woman with the ready smile? Where is the easygoing, fun-loving wife, always quick with a joke and a happy laugh? She has somehow vanished, replaced by a scowling, bitter woman, quick to reproach and criticise.

I can't help but feel sorry for him, but I also feel sorry for myself and the situation I now find us in. And I really don't know what to do about it.

In the late spring and summer the farm is beautiful and I am determined, no matter how miserable I am feeling, to try to make the most of it. Our first season of living there is well before the drought sets in so the paddocks are smothered with lush green pasture and both the dam and creek are bubbling with cool, clear water. Behind the old hall is an area that has been used for decades as a vegetable garden, and when I slip a spade into the soil it is like butter, rich and dark and teeming with worms. There is a stand of three mature walnut trees, probably more than sixty years old, but in that first season they bear no fruit because of the late frost that hit during the flowering time, cutting the tips and turning the canopy black. The trees have recovered and are fully clothed in fresh healthy foliage, with the promise of a good crop next season. Because walnuts are one of the most important crops in southwest France I am pleased to have three magnificent trees of my own. In poor rural areas of the Lot, ownership of even one good walnut tree is to be prized, and you often see very old women in pinafores with baskets gathering the fallen nut capsules in the early autumn. Perhaps that will be me in a few years' time.

Along the back fenceline I discover a long, deep drift of brilliant yellow daffodils, so plentiful that I am able to pick them by the bucketful to decorate the house. Their cheerfulness helps to lift my spirits, which are still wildly out of control. At this stage I start to conduct a constant and exhausting inner dialogue with myself, arguing the case for and against continuing my relationship with the man from Toulouse. We have almost daily contact and this keeps the feeling between us alive. I wonder whether, if we stopped communicating altogether, it would assume less significance in my life and gradually fade away. A large part of me wants to go back to feeling the way I did all those years before this happened – happy and cheerful and relatively content with my lot in life. But deep inside I know that I will never be quite the same person again. I have confronted so much and brought it out in the open. I can no longer just bury my feelings and pretend that everything is fine. And, of course, the other part of me relishes the fact that this man is so enamoured of me, wants me, and is prepared to take risks so that we can eventually be together, even if it is just for a few stolen moments.

At the farm I decide that I am not going to fall into the trap of creating a large and time-consuming ornamental garden, even though I know that this is what most people expect of me. Garden clubs phone and asked if they can come and visit – by the busload – and I am open and welcoming to them, explaining that what they will see are lots of green paddocks and well established trees but no deep flower beds of perennials and old roses or herbaceous borders overflowing with rare alpine treasures, as in my previous garden. What they will see here is a real farm with a few old wilting hydrangeas and many, many weeds. I host a few morning and afternoon teas with groups and they love exploring the old house and hearing its history, then make encouraging comments about how beautiful the garden will be once I 'get going' with it. But I am determined not to.

I do, however, intend to establish a good-sized vegetable garden to grow all the wonderful produce that I have enjoyed buying in the markets and cooking for friends in our little village house in Frayssinet. Being in a cold climate, the garden is suitable for all sorts of berry fruits – raspberries, blueberries, boysenberries, currants and strawberries. Artichokes grow brilliantly here, as do asparagus, rhubarb and all the perennials that need a winter chill to be at their best. I also intend to grow herbs as well as winter and summer vegetables, although the locals inform me that getting tomatoes to ripen in one season is not always possible.

'Never plant your tomatoes until the day after the Melbourne Cup,' one old-timer tells me with conviction. 'The late frost will get them every time.'

I gradually start to meet our neighbours living in the immediate vicinity. Robert and Sue, who have restored the old inn just down the road, arrive one afternoon with a bottle of wine and a copy of an old photograph of our house, taken possibly around 1920. The original owner, Mabel Walshaw, had been Robert's great-aunt and he knows every square inch of the house and the farmland surrounding it, having spent so much time here in his childhood. His family is one of the largest and oldest in the district. They have lived here for four generations and he is the oldest of six sons who have all remained, more or less, as neighbours. Robert works in town but also farms the land around the old inn and is a part-time beekeeper, a tradition maintained from the previous generation. Sue grows the best peonies in the district, huge white, pink and crimson flowerheads – peonies are considered 'difficult' plants to cultivate in most regions of Australia. Here the winter chill creates exactly the right growing environment, and seeing Sue's magnificent collection of peonies in full bloom, I am sorely tempted to try growing them myself. But I resist. Robert and Sue quickly become firm friends and we wander back and forth to each other's homes for casual evening meals together. The inn they have restored would have been the halfway staging post for travellers between Lithgow and Bathurst. They have almost completed a function hall on one side, with accommodation that will eventually become a bed and breakfast. The house is perfect for it.

I also meet David's soulmate, Russell, late one afternoon when we are taking a stroll around the paddock that adjoins our two properties. Russell has a beer in his hand when he comes to the fence to greet us, and puts it on the ground so he can shake my hand vigorously. He's a good-looking man in his early fifties with slightly wild eyes and a humorous turn of phrase.

'Take your sunglasses off so I can see your eyes,' he says without any hint of rudeness.

I oblige and smile at him. He takes both my hands in his and gazes deep into my eyes. 'You're lovely,' he says, which makes David laugh and me blush.

'It's a pleasure to meet you,' I say, trying to change the subject. 'David has told me a lot about you.'

'I'm sure he has,' says Russell. 'You probably won't think it's a pleasure for long. Most people don't like me much when they get to know me.'

'Nonsense,' I say. 'Come over and have a beer or a cup of tea with us any time you like.'

We talk a little about his organic farm, in which he grows rows of brilliant scarlet rhubarb and huge heads of garlic between the piles of rusting rubbish that are scattered over most of his paddocks. He uses geese as natural insect control, and they also help to keep down the grass that grows wildly in and around the old car wrecks and rusty fridges. Russell has numerous and quite high-level horticultural qualifications and is aware of my work as a gardening writer. But his life has been sorely affected by alcoholism which, at the moment, he assures us, he has under control.

'I've just done two programs in town that help problem drinkers,' he tells me. 'They've really helped,' he adds, reaching for another beer.

I instantly like Russell, even though I can see that he's more than a little eccentric. There's something lovable and very vulnerable about him and David and I agree that having him as a neighbour far outweighs the disadvantage of his unsightly rubbish collection. When we first saw the 'Steptoe and Son' state of his property we planned to plant a thick screening hedge to obliterate it, but now, having met Russell, we think his eclectic mess adds to the appeal of our mutual surroundings.

There are two younger couples in the street. Across the road is a couple with three boys approximately the same age as my older grandsons, and in a small cottage next door a younger couple who have a baby girl about the same age as little Gus. They are all friendly and welcoming and I feel almost immediately accepted into the community.

Robert and Sue have an old tractor and they offer to turn over the old vegetable garden so that I can get going with my ambitious plans to create a French-style potager. When I indicate the size of the area I want ploughed Robert looks bemused.

'You planning to feed all of Bathurst, are you?' he says.

'Well, I do have a large family,' I say in my defence. 'And I am planning to grow perennials like artichokes and asparagus and potatoes which take up a lot of space.'

For me it's an utter luxury to have this much space to play with, even though I know, that cultivating such a large vegetable garden will involve an enormous amount of work.

I am planning to try to make our Australian farm as close to the model of a French farm as possible. This means I want to concentrate only on plants and animals that provide food for the table. The French have an entirely different attitude towards gardening, stemming from centuries of poverty where no resource was wasted for frivolous decorative purposes. When you talk to a French person about their 'jardin' they will automatically assume you are referring to their potager. It all comes down to the cost of the plants and the fertiliser and water that is used to keep those plants alive. French farmers who don't have their own independent water supply are on a 'user pays' system and wouldn't dream of splashing costly water onto prissy perennial borders. Potted pelargoniums and begonias are okay, as are roses planted against the old stone walls. At least they are relatively drought-resistant. Because eating is so important to the French, growing good things to eat is also a priority. I intend taking the same approach, and scour the rural newspaper classifieds, looking for breeding stock of muscovy ducks and geese that I intend to use for meat as well as the pure white fat that is so highly prized in French cuisine.

'It won't be long,' I say to David with great enthusiasm,

'before we are frying our own potatoes in our own goose fat.'

Russell soons becomes a regular visitor, hopping over the fence for a beer in the late afternoon and offering all sorts of advice and help for various jobs that need to be done around the farm. About 5.30 one afternoon, he calls by when David and I are still working, he on a script and me on a magazine article. Russell brings a large bunch of glorious rhubarb – he never comes empty-handed – but we don't invite him to stay for a drink because we haven't quite come to the end of our working day.

'Come and have a drink tomorrow,' I say to him, 'when we are not so busy.'

That evening, after nightfall, we see the flashing lights of a police vehicle, driving along the old highway at the back of the property. We don't think much about it, but on the local radio news the next morning we hear of a local man being killed in a road accident the night before. Again, we don't think much about it except to wonder who it might have been. Later that day, a neighbour phones and tells us it was Russell. We are totally devastated by the news. Apparently, not long after he left our place he took his utility truck and drove towards town. The tailgate fell off and he pulled his vehicle over to the side of the road. It was just before dusk when visibility is poor. As he went to retrieve the tailgate, a large fourwheel drive came down the highway, hauling a horse trailer. It was the trailer that hit Russell, and he was killed instantly.

'If only we'd asked him to stay for a drink,' I lament, 'this may never have happened.' I feel dreadful.

But that's a stupid thing to say. It was just his time, Russell's time to go. He was a true eccentric and, even though we have only just got to know him and appreciate his funny ways, we shall miss him. But his unexpected death upsets me more than I expect, perhaps because I am in a sensitive frame of mind. David, too, is hit hard by the news, and when we go for our regular late-afternoon walk now we invariably stand at the spot where we used to chat to Russell over the fence and look sadly at his collection of rusting rubble. I'm not sure what's going through David's mind, but I know for me it's a salient reminder that life is very fragile and that it can be cut short at any moment – after all, Russell was exactly my age.

One of David's responses to the possibility of my having a relationship with another man is to take a long hard look at himself, at the way he looks, the way he feels and the way he often behaves around the house. Not only is he overweight and lacking in energy, he is often grumpy and negative, and these personality characteristics are hard for me to live with. It's very easy for him to slip into a trough, especially as he is by nature a little on the dour side, so he decides, wisely, to turn things around. He enrols at the gym in Bathurst and starts again on his old exercise regime. As before, the results are amazing. Within weeks his former fitness levels start to return and his whole attitude to life improves. I am not sure whether it is the endorphins released during a workout, but he becomes addicted to his daily 'fix' of exercise and combines it well with other helpful routines. After the gym he does the household shopping, pays the bills, visits the post office and does all the other irritating administrative tasks associated with running the farm. When he comes home each day he has a smile on his face and is often clutching a bottle of champagne or some other little gift for me. It is like living with a different man, and it certainly helps with the rekindling of our relationship. All the good things are coming back. He often phones me to say he's about to leave town for the twenty-minute drive back to the farm. I light the little fire in our bedroom and have a bath and when he returns we spend most of the afternoon in bed. It's no wonder I have little time for gardening.

We spend many pleasant evenings sitting on the front verandah, sipping a beer and looking down at the patchwork of coloured foliage in the arboretum. We are of like mind on one thing. Neither of us wants to tear apart what we have spent thirty-one years creating. Not the bricks and mortar of our two homes, the farm here in Australia and the village house in France, but the enormous investment we have made in our large and happy family, the emotional investment, the love that is there for all to see. I can't seem to help the way that I am feeling, so unsettled and so restless. My mind still flashes frequently to thoughts of the man from Toulouse. But I am determined that somehow this marriage will survive.

Through all this difficult stage of our relationship David remains supportive. He could easily have lost patience with my instability. Many men, in the same situation, would have assumed that the marriage was over and would have taken flight. I wouldn't have blamed him if he had. But he doesn't. From time to time he shows his frustration and sometimes even his anger at my erratic behaviour, but he stays and tries to improve the situation by being mostly upbeat and positive. It's a strange role reversal. After all those decades of my keeping things on an even keel, suddenly he's assuming the role of holding everything together.

20

 Every weekend the children come to the farm, bringing their own children and their dogs. Our two younger sons, Aaron and Ethan, have both agreed to work around the farm in return for some financial help with establishing their own homes and businesses. Ethan is establishing a wholesale nursery in one of the paddocks behind the big old shed and, with a partner, intends to grow tubestock of local native plants for large-scale bush regeneration projects. Aaron, who lives and works in Mudgee with his wife Lorna and two small children, loves the farm and should probably have been brought up on one himself. He wears a battered bush hat and thrashes the old 'paddock basher' Dodge ute around the back blocks of the farm, cutting up wood for the fires and repairing the wobbly fences. Between them the boys have an impressive list of horticultural qualifications and have followed in my footsteps in their love of nature, the soil and growing things. It's very gratifying.

I spend most of the weekends playing with my grandchildren

and preparing huge family meals that we eat under the cherry tree if the weather is warm, or at the vast table in the formal dining room when it's cold. The house is fully set up for small children, with cots and highchairs and bath toys. I have even started to accumulate a collection of 'farm clothes' for the children, including stacks of gumboots and spare outfits for the inevitable accidents when they get smothered in mud or fall in the creek. These weekends are sheer bliss, and I realise that the only time I feel truly, deeply happy is when I am surrounded by all the little ones. I feel safe, and needed, and well loved when there are six small people swinging around my ankles. How can this be so? By this stage of my life I should have got over this urgent need to be loved and needed. But I haven't. When I am here alone with David I feel somehow hollow and wanting. When the entire gang is around, laughing and talking full belt and drinking beer and wrangling with the children, I feel like my old self again.

My daughter and daughters-in-law all love to cook and these weekend get-togethers are triumphs of teamwork. When I first returned from France I lugged back heavy tins of confit du canard (preserved duck) for which I paid exorbitant excess baggage charges because Air France had decided to start weighing every passenger's hand luggage. When we finally decide to open them I tell the children this will be a very expensive lunch, but worth every mouthful.

We start with an aperitif called Fenelon, which is very typical of the southwest of France. It's made from splash of eau de noix (walnut liquor) and a splash of cassis (blackcurrant liquor), topped up with dry red wine. I have found a recipe on the Internet for making eau de noix from green walnuts and I plan to start a batch the following season if our trees escape the frost. One less thing to carry back from France.

Next we have a clear soup made from good chicken stock, just as it's made by Mme Murat in Pomarede. It's light and fragrant and, instead of filling the pot with remnants of stale bread, I provide crusty fresh bread so people can do their own dipping. The broth doesn't even need salt or pepper, so rich and clear is the flavour.

We skip the charcuterie course because I realise that these unaccustomed bellies simply won't have space for the main attraction of the meal – the duck. Confit is sold in all the markets in France, displayed in glass cases alongside other savoury deli-cacies. Our local butcher in Frayssinet, M Didier, also has portions of preserved duck in his window – coated with a thick white film that is the goose fat in which the duck was cooked and therefore preserved. The tinned confit isn't quite up to that standard, but it's still mouth-watering. Cooking it is simple. I heat up several large cast iron frying pans then scrape away most of the fat. Some of the fat goes into another large flat frying pan, for sautéing the potatoes, and the rest I store in an airtight jar in the fridge for later use. It's like precious gold.

The duck portions just need to be heated through, then turned so that the skin becomes deep brown and crispy. It only takes about ten minutes. Meanwhile, the potatoes, which have been parboiled, are being fried to a crisp golden-brown. Nothing on earth tastes as good as these potatoes cooked in goose or duck fat. They are sublime.

We don't have any other vegetables with the meal, just the duck and potatoes, and the table is silent as we crunch our way through this feast. The only abstainer is Lynne, now heavily pregnant, who developed an aversion to rich French food early in her pregnancy and is still feeling more than a little queasy. She has grilled fish instead.

After a lengthy pause, more wine and conversation, we have cheese. It's excellent local cheese, but not as flavoursome as the unpasteurised camembert and Cantal that I have grown addicted to in France. Lastly, I produce a rich duck-egg baked custard served with strawberries that have been soaking for several hours in sweet red wine. It's a struggle to get up and leave the table.

Our grandchildren seem to enjoy adventurous eating and join enthusiastically in these gargantuan Sunday repasts. They are developing sophisticated tastes and often ask for special meals of rabbit stew with prunes or barbecued octopus or char-grilled capsicum. They even enjoy the vegetables normally loathed by small people, so I plant rows and rows of broad beans and cabbages and brussels sprouts, knowing full well that they will be widely appreciated, even by the two-year-olds. It makes me very happy to feed them and see them enjoy their food. The way they belt around the farm after lunch, riding bikes or swinging from the gum tree, reassures me that there's no chance they will become overweight and sluggish like children given a diet of fast food, computer games and television. They can stuff themselves with goose fat and broad beans to their heart's content and still be as lean and lithe as children are meant to be.

As a young mother I used to think that a child's environment was the most important factor in determining their character and future happiness. I believed that my own personality had been strongly shaped by my childhood and this made me deter-mined to give my own children the happiest and most carefree childhood possible. Over the decades I have changed my view somewhat: now I believe that children are born with an imprint of personality that will stay with them forever. The way they are brought up will make a huge difference to them in terms of confidence and feeling loved, but I now believe that people are what they are. My four children are so different in personality and character that I can hardly believe they all grew up under the same roof. Now I am watching my seven little grandchildren emerge as individuals and it gives me great joy to develop a very special and personal relationship with each of them. I try to have them to stay overnight one at a time so that I can concentrate on that particular child – it's like a madhouse when they are all here at once, noisily vying for attention.

As the farm has some good sheds for keeping poultry, I expand my chicken flock of brown Isers (French hens that are particularly good layers) and purchase a muscovy drake and three ducks from a local breeder. They are an excellent line, having won numerous firsts at the Royal Easter Show, but I make the mistake of putting them in with the chickens instead of isolating them in their own separate area. There's a lot of squawking and fussing but I figure it will settle down when they get used to each other.

Some old neighbours from the mountains ask if we can provide a home for their muscovy drake, affectionately known as Laurie. Short, they tell me, for Duck L'Orange. They arrive with him in a large travelling cage and he emerges in a foul mood, with his beady eyes angrily surveying the territory.

'He has a bit of a personality disorder,' my friends tell me sheepishly. 'He sometimes gives people a nip, but he means well. He's really very affectionate.'

They leave quickly, saying they'll come back and visit him from time to time. They never do.

Laurie is anything but affectionate. He's a demented and confused creature who has been reared as a child instead of a drake, and is accustomed to being picked up and carried around and kissed and fondled. At his original home, I later discover, he was allowed to wander in and out of the house, and his favourite pastime was gazing at his own reflection in a large gilt-edged mirror. Most chickens and ducks and geese avoid close contact with humans. When you go into the poultry yards they move away while the water is being changed and the hoppers filled with fresh grain and pellets. Not so Laurie. He immediately sidles up to anyone who enters and hisses loudly, jerking his large head back and forth. If he isn't given attention immediately he leans forward and viciously pecks the skin on your shins. Even if you do pay heed to his advances by stroking his head or picking him up, he's just as inclined to repay your kindness with another sharp peck. He is, in fact, a totally unlovable fat bully of a bird, and I can understand why my Leura friends were so keen to offload him. I decide not to put him in with my muscovy breeding stock, but I notice he spends most of the day pacing up and down the fence that separates the yards, hissing and trying to goad the 'well-adjusted' muscovy drake into a confrontation.

When Miriam and her family visit the farm they usually bring their Jack Russell terrier Ulysses. He's a good-natured dog and an excellent companion for the children but he has one major fault. He is overwhelmingly attracted to the notion of killing poultry, and as he emerges from the car each Sunday he makes an immediate beeline for the chicken runs. We aim to keep him safely indoors during the visit but, as the children are constantly going in and out of the house, he always manages to duck between their feet and slip under the big gate into the paddock where the ducks are swimming on the dam. Usually the first we know is the panic-stricken quacking that tells us the ducks are in danger and en masse we run to the rescue. The scene is one of ducks swimming wildly in circles with Ulysses paddling as furiously as his short legs will work, which fortunately isn't very fast. From time to time he actually manages to catch one by the throat, so when he is visiting I decide the only way of maintaining calm is to muzzle him from the moment he gets out of the car. Nothing is more pathetic than a dog that is muzzled. It must be the origin of the expression 'hangdog,' because Ulysses sits with eyes downcast and hunched shoulders, looking utterly miserable. If we weaken and remove the muzzle he shakes his head, rubs his nose along the grass then instantly takes off in search of some poor bird to attack.

The pasture in the paddocks is growing at such a pace that we need some livestock to graze and keep it down or it will be waist-high by the end of summer. A neighbour has a large mixed herd of cows and poddy calves and we agree to agist a few in return for some rudimentary fencing work. He turns up with a large truck on Sunday morning when all the grandchildren are visiting, and they watch with delight as this odd little herd of seven is unloaded through our small cattle yard. The friendliest is an old white cow called Snowy, heavy with possibly her eighth or ninth calf. Miriam's son Theo, who is three at the time, is enraptured with these large, slow-moving animals and I spend half my time taking him up into the back paddocks to look for them. When we get close, Theo is nervous and hides behind my legs, unwilling to hand-feed them as the other children do. But he just loves them.

'I'm going to be a cowboy when I grow up, Mutie,' he informs me, showing me a photograph in a book of a man on horseback lassoing a steer with massive curved horns.

It's a curious career choice for a small boy who's not only frightened of cows but also terrified of horses. Every time we try to get near the horses at the local agricultural show, Theo starts to sob and asks to be taken further away. Still, I let him have his dreams.

The three pregnant cows are all due to calve around the same time and I keep a close eye on them, checking first thing in the morning and again in the late afternoon. I have no knowledge or experience of livestock, but I feel confident that they will give birth without any trouble, just as women do if they are left alone to get on with it and not hooked up to machines or knocked out with painkillers.

Early one afternoon I wander around to the back paddock, where the grass is very long. I see the cows grazing in the distance then suddenly come upon two tiny, damp calves curled up asleep in the long grass. There are still remnants of afterbirth around them, and as I approach they wake up and bleat. The two mothers, one of them Snowy, immediately bellow loudly and come towards me in a protective manner. I move away quietly and watch with delight as the two newborns stand under their mothers and feed. Miriam brings the boys out to see the babies that very afternoon.

Both are female and I allow the boys to name them – Flossy and Luce. A few days later the third calf is born, a small grey male. They call him Bubby Gorgeous. Having baby animals around is lovely, and I am happy for the children to have the experience of watching the calves and being able to handle them. We have a huge old apple tree, laden with fruit, and we feed the windfalls to the cattle. By the time the calves are big enough to eat the fruit they are also wise enough to notice us heading towards the tree with baskets and they gambol with pleasure as they cross the paddock towards the gate where we feed them. It's a lot of fun.

Our chicken run has two roosters, which is one more than is strictly required. The brown and white speckled rooster is timid but extremely handsome, with a brilliant red comb and graceful arching tail feathers. The white rooster, a leghorn, is just as handsome but devilishly aggressive; he takes any opportunity to strike, targeting small children in particular with his wicked spurs. When we go in to gather eggs in the afternoon he often flies at the children, aiming for the head, specifically the eyes, and I decide that he is too dangerous to keep in the flock. We shall have to eat him.

The following weekend Aaron neatly despatches him with a sharp axe and I sit on a plastic chair under the cherry tree, plucking him for the next day's lunch. Aaron's son Hamish, aged four, watches the killing of the rooster without concern and is fascinated by the plucking process, standing close to me and chatting cheerily while I remove the last of the fine feathers from the bird's belly. He asks for a couple of long tail feathers to play with and I oblige. I think it's good that children understand where food comes from and don't feel squeamish about it. I then enlarge the vent with a sharp knife so I can remove the gizzards, which I do by hand. The bird is still warm and very soft. Hamish is particularly interested in this part of the process but, as I plunge my hand into the cavity, I force air inside the bird and it travels all the way up the windpipe to the small voicebox, which is still intact. The headless rooster promptly crows loudly in his distinctive, pre-decapitation voice. A look of total horror comes over Hamish's face and he takes off towards the house at full pace, dropping the tail feathers on the ground. Lorna brings him back outside a few moments later and I explain to him what has happened. But it doesn't reassure him much. He asks me repeatedly, 'Is the rooster dead, Mutie? Is the rooster really dead?'

But when it comes to the crunch the following day, Hamish doesn't hesitate, enjoying a thick slice of the rooster's breast with baked potatoes and rich gravy. So do the other small boys (I usually have to cook two or three chickens when the whole mob comes to lunch). Hamish happily tells his cousins about the dead rooster who could still crow.

Later that afternoon when we are gathering eggs, young Theo leans over and speaks confidentially to one of the plump young hens. 'Ha, ha, ha,' he says. 'I ate your Dad!'

I guess that none of them has been traumatised by the realities of life on the farm.

Our cats have become outside cats, which is more appropriate on a farm. Because of the flies I can't leave a window open so that they can hop in and out at will, and because they are all quite geriatric they can't be left inside with the doors closed – they will make a mess on the carpet. I set up the laundry with baskets and boxes filled with old towels and blankets, and they quickly adapt to this more rugged lifestyle. The oldest cat is a black and white male that the children named Marilyn, after the famous actress, because when he was a tiny kitten we thought he was a female. The name stuck, but his personality never quite matched his effervescent namesake. A few months after arriving at the farm, Marilyn starts to look very scrawny and drink a lot of water, a sure sign of the kidney disease that seems to be the downfall of most domestic moggies. One morning he doesn't show up for his breakfast and I spend most of the day looking for him. I take a torch and go under the house, and together David and I scout around the garden and look in the shed, but Marilyn isn't to be seen.

David is convinced that he has taken himself off somewhere to die but I don't give up, spending the next few days searching and calling, even into the night. After several weeks we feel certain that Marilyn has done exactly what David predicted. One weekend when the boys are working in the toolshed, sharpening the blades of the chainsaw to collect more wood for my fuel stove, they notice huge blowflies going in and out under the door of the locked storage shed where most of our office equipment and books is still stored in boxes. Then they detect the most hideous smell.

'Think we've found your cat, Mum,' says Aaron, and fetches the key for the shed.

Sure enough. Marilyn must have crawled through a small gap in the timber door and simply curled up and died. But that was weeks ago and in this hot weather he has turned into black and white soup. What follows is funnier, in a macabre way, than a circus. There are three adult males – David, Aaron and Ethan – and none of them is capable of dealing with the dead cat in its current condition.

'I'll dig the hole,' says Ethan, grabbing a spade and getting as far away from the shed as possible.

David paces the lawn, still in his nightshirt, muttering and mumbling into his whiskers and wringing his hands in despair. Aaron puts on a brave face and tries to scoop the remains into a box with a flat shovel, but immediately starts to heave. It takes an eternity for them to complete the task, with David doing the worst of it in the end, and I am left with the grisly job of cleaning up and getting rid of the maggots that have multiplied into thousands. The shed smells frightful for weeks, and that particular Sunday nobody feels much like lunch.

Being in the midst of such a large and lively family and distracted by all the tasks of running the farm helps me cope with my mental confusion. I realise that this is the way I have coped for most of my adult life: by creating an environment around me which is so busy and demanding that I don't have the time or energy to think too deeply about how I am feeling. But now, in the middle of the night, my dilemma returns to haunt me. When the children and grandchildren have gone home at the end of the day, after dinner and a few glasses of wine I am left alone with David and my thoughts, knowing that I am feeling far from happy.

21

A couple of months after Christmas the long-awaited letter from my sister Margaret finally arrives. After the brief card she wrote acknowledging the copy of *Au Revoir* I sent there was a long, long silence, and I was seriously worried that she would never write again. Perhaps her childhood memories are so traumatic that she doesn't care to relive them in any form – neither the written nor the spoken word. Perhaps her need to divorce herself totally from our family is so strong that my reappearance, after fifty years, is just too much for her to stand.

But not so. Margaret's letter is long and friendly, handwritten and covering ten pages. She tells me with humour and some pride about her full and happy life, the life she made for herself after walking out the front door of our overcrowded and unhappy flat on her eighteenth birthday. There is little reference to the pain of her childhood, just lots of good news about her extensive travels and her career. When she left home she was on a teacher's college scholarship and training at East Sydney Tech to be an art teacher. It was a struggle but, by working at nights and weekends, usually in factories, she managed to support herself until she completed her degree. She then worked in a couple of country high schools as an art teacher: for several years in Cooma, in the Snowy Mountains, and then at Dubbo. In the 1960s she went to England to teach and from there she travelled to Canada, where again she taught art in rural schools. Along the way she decided to upgrade her qualifications and completed two masters degrees, eventually undertaking a PhD in art education. Margaret didn't marry until her mid-thirties and she and her husband Ken, also a teacher, don't have children. Margaret embraced Ken's large extended family and eventually, when they both retired, they built a farmhouse and established a commercial kiwi fruit farm on glorious Vancouver Island, where they still live.

Margaret sends me a photograph of herself, now aged in her late sixties, standing in her garden wearing a straw hat. She looks so much like me, only with grey hair, and I am amazed at the parallels in our lives. She loves her garden and is an enthusiastic producer of compost. She loves to cook and fills her pantry shelves with jams and jellies and preserves, just as I have done for years. She and Ken love to travel and they have spent many happy holidays with friends painting village scenes in France. Not just anywhere in France, but in exactly the same region of France that we so love and where we own our little house.

The hair on the back of my neck stands up. This is my sister that I don't know. She left our home when I was fourteen months old and made a totally different life for herself. Yet here she is, so like me in so many ways. She obviously had a burning need to achieve too, hence her long string of academic qualifications.

She must be a kindred spirit. I read her letter over and over, soaking up her handwriting, drinking in every word.

For the first time in months I feel really happy. So much has happened in my life these last twelve months – the move from Leura, the entanglement with the man from Toulouse which has created so much confusion in my mind, the sheer hard physical work of setting up the farm, the launch of the book and the overwhelming reaction to it, the rediscovery of my long-lost sister and my inner struggle with my relationship with David. I feel quite drained emotionally.

In January we have our first big party at the farm and I am thankful for the large community hall that will accommodate the seventy or so guests we invite. My half-brother Jon who lives in the small town of Warialda in northern New South Wales will be seventy, and I decide to round up as many of his and our relatives and old working colleagues as possible and have a lunchtime gathering in early January. By email, phone, fax and snail mail I manage to track down five of his cousins on his mother's side of the family, the Fannings, who came originally from Melbourne, where our father, Theo, met Jon's mother, Veronica, back in the early 1930s. These cousins range in age from mid-forties to late fifties and are scattered around the countryside but, because they've all stayed in close touch with each other, it's easy to find them and they are all happy to be invited.

I also contact some of our Moody cousins, the various offspring of my father's brother Rollie, who was a well-known journalist of his era. Now, if my father was a cad and a womaniser and a drunk, his brother Rollie left him for dead. Rollie married several times and fathered illegitimate children in between – well, at least one that we know of. His first wife had two sons. His second wife (my darling Aunty Jeanne, who died two years ago) had three sons and a daughter. Then there was a daughter out of wedlock, which caused a scandal at the newspaper where they all worked. Who knows what after that. Rollie's preferred *modus operandi* was to have two women pregnant at the same time. Initially, neither would be aware of the other but eventually he would try to move them all in together in a communal living arrangement. He succeeded at least once in convincing a wife that the mistress and baby should move in. It didn't work out, as one would expect, and in the end Rollie fled back to Melbourne, abandoning all the children and their mothers. He offered no financial, physical or emotional support to any of them. Attempts had been made over the years to link up the half-brothers and sisters, and I had met some of them at a small but happy reunion in Sydney the previous year. Now I want them all to come to Jon's party; this means that at least two of them – half-sisters – will be meeting each other for the first time. It makes me think of my own tenuous link with Margaret. What a tangled family these Moodys are, with so much pain and confusion caused by two egotistical, self-centred brothers.

I also manage to round up various members of my mother's family, children and grandchildren of her brothers and sisters. A lot of these cousins are also fairly wild and wacky, so I can tell it's going to be a spirited gathering.

All my children and their partners come to help, grand-children and dogs in tow, and we prepare a huge buffet lunch with lots of wine and beer. I'm not too sure about the Fannings, but the Moodys and the Angels (my mother's clan) are partial to a drop or two, so the fridges are well stocked.

It turns out to be the most wonderful day for everyone. All these people connected by the common thread of the notorious Theo and Rollie Moody come together to celebrate the birthday of the oldest member of his generation – dear Jon. I have a vivid memory of Lynne, by now almost nine months pregnant, zipping in and out of the house with huge platters of cold meats and salads and cheeses. Miriam and Lorna and my stepson Tony's wife, Simone, are also kitchen slaves. It's very much all hands to the pump. The children, as young as little Gus, who is now crawling, have no idea what the party is all about but join in the fun and gets lots of hugs and kisses from second cousins and distant in-laws whom they have never met. It is a couple of hours before the two half-sisters, one in her forties, one in her fifties, work their way round to talking to each other, but by mid-afternoon I see them sitting together in a huddle, laughing and talking. Jon is slightly overawed by it all. We make speeches and there is a huge birthday cake. The party goes on well into the evening, so it's just as well the fridge is well stocked.

Next morning, as we tidy up and say goodbye to the last of the cousins, Jon sits on the back verandah and reflects on the gathering.

'You know, Mary,' he says with a sigh, 'I've never had a birthday party before.'

It was a long time to wait.

Ten days after Jon's party Ethan and Lynne produce a beautiful baby girl. Isabella Rosa is tiny but perfectly formed and has, to my delight, a crown of bright red hair. We are overjoyed to welcome another girl into the family – an ally for her sixteen-month-old cousin Ella Mary – in among this large bunch of boisterous boys. Now, when the whole family comes to the farm for Sunday lunch, there are seventeen of us. I can't believe that at 52 I already have seven grandchildren. It's a tight squeeze even for our large dining room table, and the preparation of food is a massive undertaking. Just as well most of us are keen to cook – it's probably because we are also very keen to eat good food. It's a joyous time.

One afternoon there's a knock at the kitchen door and a slim young woman introduces herself as Sue. She lives at nearby Kirkconnell and wonders if I would like to get involved in a community concert they are planning to stage in a few weeks' time. While I am always enthusiastic about helping out in community events, I can't imagine what I could possibly contribute to a concert. I can't sing,

I don't play a musical instrument and I have never been very keen on poetry recitals. After some discussion I volunteer to try doing a small comedy skit impersonating Peter Cundall, the larger-than-life main presenter on the gardening program that I was involved with for so many years. Peter is quite a character with his thick Mancunian accent and overwhelming enthusiasm for all things related to gardening and the environment. He is well loved by all the regular fans of the show, and even those who aren't regular viewers will recognise my take-off because he's a bit of a television legend. He is well known as a ruthless man with a pruning saw and I have developed a small routine, only ever performed at visits to gardening clubs, where I take off his approach to pruning a lemon tree. Massacre would be a better word. I take a lemon tree in a pot and, while explaining the technique of restoring it to good health and vigour through pruning, I reduce it to the size of a petunia seedling. Sue is most enthusiastic about my idea but she also enquires, a little tentatively, if I would be interested in taking part in the can-can chorus.

I protest that I couldn't possibly dance the can-can. I don't know the steps. I've never done it before. I'd make a complete fool of myself.

'We are famous for being bad,' she says. 'It's a really easy routine. Why not just come to our rehearsal this afternoon and see what you think?'

Much to David's horror, I set off for the new community hall in the late afternoon and, after an hour of kicking and sweating and screaming, I feel I have started to come to grips with the rhythm of the dance. It's great fun.

We have time for only four rehearsals before the night of the concert but, as Sue has rightly pointed out, it's an easy routine

to remember and we are all very enthusiastic. Our ages range
from early twenties to late fifties and we are all basically fit
although not quite as glamorous and sexy as Nicole Kidman in
Moulin Rouge. Some of the younger women can do cartwheels,
which adds plenty of colour and movement to the routine. I
think it's hilarious, though David has grave reservations about
the whole idea. Having worked professionally in the entertainment industry for forty years, he feels uncomfortable with
amateur performances. For years I used to hoot at the Saturday
night 'Red Faces' segment on 'Hey, Hey it's Saturday' but David
would leave the room covered in embarrassment. He simply
can't stand people making fools of themselves by being 'bad'
performers. I have a totally different viewpoint. I think there's
a desire in all of us to get up and perform, and it doesn't really
matter if we are good or bad, as long as we are having fun. David
has a fear of people 'dying' in front of a live audience so I hope,
for his sake, that I don't fall over and make a complete spectacle
of myself.

The community concert is a most entertaining event. The
hall doesn't have a stage, but the tables are cleared to the side,
leaving an open space for the performances. Everyone from the
community rocks along, bringing their children and bottles of
wine and beer and plates of nibbles to enjoy during the show.
The organisers have put together a lavish supper for afterwards
and the idea is that anyone and everyone is welcome to get up
and 'have a go'. And they do.

There are small rock groups and violin players and kids doing
poetry and singing pop songs, there are line dancers and stand-
up comedians and soloists who throw their heart and soul into
every note. Not every performance is a winner, but the crowd's

enthusiasm is overwhelming and the atmosphere is very friendly. I love every moment, even when it's my turn to get up, dressed in daggy old gardening clothes and gumboots, to do my silly skit. It goes down well and I spy several of my grandsons standing in the doorway looking a little embarrassed at their grandmother centre stage, hacking a lemon tree into small pieces and shouting 'blooming marvellous' in a funny accent.

The last act of the night is the can-can and we all crowd into the ladies' loo to get dressed and apply our exaggerated make-up. There hasn't been time for a dress rehearsal, but we are all wearing full skirts and skimpy tops and fishnet tights, with bright red feathers pinned into our hair. Over my fishnets I decide to wear a pair of saucy red knickers, vaguely see-through and with lots of lace. We run onto the stage energetically and the routine goes off like clockwork. It brings the house down and to cries of 'More! More!' we somehow manage an encore. It's exhausting. After supper and more wine we all stagger back to the farm, agreeing that the community concert is definitely one local event not to be missed. Even David agrees.

Next morning the phone rings quite early. It's Sue, our can-can mistress, and we have a good laugh about how brilliant the concert was and how well received our can-can was by the audience.

She asks me, rather sheepishly, 'And what were you wearing over your fishnet stockings?'

'Just some red lacy knickers,' I say.

'Yes, but what were you wearing under them?'

'Nothing,' I reply. 'Just the tights and the knickers.'

'I thought so,' she says with a laugh. 'Several people phoned this morning to ask. It caused a lot of interest.'

'Well,' I said defensively, 'I thought red lacy knickers would be appropriate. What were you all wearing?'

'Black bicycle shorts,' she said. 'That's what we always wear.'

Whoops!

Nobody told me that modesty was the order of the night, and I couldn't see what the others were wearing because we were dancing in a straight line. Only here a few months and already I've caused a scandal in the parish!

The family stays overnight, and on Sunday morning, as we are recovering from the night before over cups of tea and coffee, I ask little Theo if he enjoyed the concert.

'Yes, Mutie,' he says, beaming. 'It was great.'

'And what was your favourite bit?' I ask.

'I liked that bit when you showed everyone your arse,' he says.

Oh dear, out of the mouths of babes . . .

After Russell's death, his tenant Frank sends a message round the village asking if anyone wants to take the geese. He genuinely hates having them around – they were Russell's foible – and he says that if nobody wants them they will be killed. I have been intrigued by the idea of breeding geese for meat and fat, as they do in France, so I readily agree to take the entire flock of twelve adult birds off Frank's hands. They are not purebred Toulouse geese, which is the variety used commercially in the Lot, but they are close enough in body size and shape to suit my purposes. The only problem will be catching them.

Frank thinks the best idea is to herd them into one of the sheds on Russell's farm late one afternoon, then come back later to grab them when it gets dark. Birds are much easier to handle when they can't see what's going on. I wait until a weekend when Aaron is there to help. Frank rounds them up and calls over the fence that they can be picked up anytime we like. We wait until about nine o'clock that night and I gather up twelve large grain sacks so that each bird can be bagged individually for safe and easy transfer. Aaron and I enter the shed by torchlight and the geese immediately become agitated, hissing and squawking and flapping their wings. We turn off the torch and discuss a plan of action: Aaron will grab the geese, one by one, by the neck, turn them over and grab their feet and together we will put them headfirst into the bags. I will then tie the bags and lay the geese in the back of my ute. The first few geese are easy to catch and bag and we think the whole operation is going smoothly, not realising that we have been catching the younger, smaller geese. The bigger they get, the stronger the fight they put up, but somehow we still manage to grapple with them and get them bagged. The shed is pitch black and smells revolting, with a thick layer of goose droppings on the floor, a lot of it very fresh and sloppy.

When Aaron gets to the last bird, obviously the dominant gander, the situation changes. The bird doesn't want to be caught, and he is large and strong enough to knock Aaron off balance. He falls backwards, quite hard, into a slurry of gooseshit, still struggling to grab the feet of the gander, who is putting up quite a fight. Aaron can't stop laughing – it's such a ridiculous situation, rolling around in the dark in muck, fighting this angry gander who is trying to peck his nose off. I'm not much better – it's after dinner and I've had a couple of glasses of wine. I find myself also slipping around the floor in hysterics, trying to control the gander, who by now is really furious. At last we get him bagged and, filthy from head to toe, we drive the flock to the shed I have prepared with a thick layer of clean straw and hoppers of water and cracked corn. The geese are quite subdued when we tip them from their bags, but David is appalled at the sight of us when we return to the house. We are still laughing and I'm in need of a long, hot shower.

The geese adapt to their new home immediately. We keep them penned for the first few days until they settle in, then let them out to graze and swim in the dam. They quickly get into the routine and I love walking up to their pen in the early morning and letting them out. They are regal creatures, walking with heads held high, then taking off in semi-flight at the top of the hill as they swoop down to the dam. Every evening they come back up to the gate and wait to be let into the pen. They walk together in an orderly fashion and show no aggression towards me – unlike other geese I have encountered over the years, who can be quite unpleasant to have around. I realise that if I am to rear them for eating they will have to be kept permanently in the pen. All this walking around and flying and swimming will make their meat dark and tough and reduce the amount of fat they produce. However, as they won't start breeding until the autumn, I decide to give them the run of the farm during the day.

In Australia, of course, we are not permitted to force-feed geese as they do in France to produce the highly prized foie gras. The RSPCA would quickly intervene if a farmer was reported for force-feeding. However, in France they have a different attitude to animals, and forcing vast quantities of grain down the throat of a goose so that its liver becomes enlarged, fatty and therefore perfect for foie gras is simply a way of life. I have watched the process of fattening geese in France and it is awful when the overstuffed birds collapse to the ground, unable to move because of the weight of the corn in their crops. The farmer justifies his production methods by saying that the actual fattening only occurs over a period of three weeks and that the geese actually like it. They line up for it. Well of course they line up – otherwise they wouldn't be fed at all. And they are always hungry birds.

The farmer also says that the process is quite natural because wild geese do exactly the same thing to themselves when preparing for the long migratory flight they undertake each year. During the weeks before migration the birds overfeed and deliberately allow their livers to become enlarged as a survival strategy to get them through the long flight ahead. The farmer assures me that only migratory birds have livers that swell up in this fashion, which is why only geese and ducks are suited to making foie gras. This means, I guess, that if you tried force-feeding a chicken or a kookaburra you wouldn't get the same result.

The actual process of making the foie gras is fascinating. I always imagined it to be a concoction, like a pâté or a terrine, with the liver mixed with other flavourings and ingredients. But no, the real foie gras is liver, just liver. Swollen and pink and fatty and fleshy. The best foie gras is processed in a tin or in glass jars when still warm, freshly extracted from the dead bird. In commercial foie gras farms they have the killing room right next to the canning room: the livers are quickly carried from where the bird has been slaughtered, put into tins and heat-processed. Jan tells me that every year she does her own foie gras. She goes to a nearby farm and buys the livers, still warm. She keeps them warm in an esky, driving home like a bat out of hell to the kitchen where warm, sterile jars are waiting. The aim is to have the lids sealed and the jars cooking before the liver has time to get cold. It all sounds brutal, but the result is so wonderful that most French people don't have any problem with the concept. I love foie gras, but only in small quantities and very occasionally. It's just too rich. I know that I won't be able to produce it in Australia, but I can still produce good meat birds with plenty of fat and make a pâté from the liver. I'm not too sure about using the gizzards, as they do in France, to make a warm salad with wilted greens and vinaigrette. I am not sure which bits of the bird go into this delicious amalgamation of flavours and textures known as salade de gesiers, so I will have to do some research next time I am in Frayssinet.

Just a few weeks after buying the flock of muscovy ducks I come home from town and find the drake in dire distress. He's half-submerged in the pond with one of his hooked claws caught in his eyelid. He has impaled himself and appears half-dead. I immediately suspect that Laurie, the maladjusted drake in the next pen, is the culprit. They have been fighting through the fence wire and somehow the well-behaved drake has managed to tangle himself up in his own claws. I gently unhook him and take him into the shed, making a warm nest of straw for him to lie still and recover. But he doesn't. He can't lift his head, and within hours he has expired.

One of the prize muscovy ducks is sitting on a clutch of eggs and I have been keeping a record. It takes thirty days for duck eggs to hatch. Chickens take only twenty days. The duck is sitting on a mixture of duck and hen eggs, which can happen when they are housed together. I should really have removed the chicken eggs but I decide to wait and see what happens. Back in Leura we had a duck that hatched chicken eggs, so I imagine that this bird may be capable of rearing a mixed flock.

Sadly, the sitting duck also meets a sudden end and I can find no explanation for it. David phones me when I am in Sydney and he sounds very upset.

'The duck sitting on the eggs is dead,' he says. 'Totally dead. And there's a tiny chicken beside her. It's just hatched out and it's cold and almost dead too.'

I tell him to put the chicken in a cardboard box and put a lamp over it so that the light bulb is quite close to the bird. It will slowly warm it.

'It's no good,' he says. 'I think it's already dead.'

'Just try, anyway,' I say. 'I will be home in a couple of hours.'

Just past Lithgow the mobile phone rings and I pull off the road. It's David, and he's elated.

'Listen to this,' he says, and puts the phone into the box so I can hear the cheep, cheep, cheeping of the yellow fluffy chick which has staged a complete recovery.

David is amazed that he has managed to save the chick. He doesn't see himself as being very practical when it comes to animals. By the time I get home the chicken is raring to go and has imprinted on David. As far as Cheepy Chicken (the name David has already given it) is concerned, David is its mother. And he is very protective. The cats must be locked out and Floyd, the Labrador, watched closely. Within days the chicken has the run of the house and can often be found snuggled up to Floyd for warmth. Whenever it hears David's voice it comes running and follows him around, cheeping and fluffing its down feathers and pecking the floor. It's hilarious, especially when David is making business calls on the portable phone, pacing up and down our long hallway with a small yellow chicken hot on his heels. For a man as fastidious as David, who dislikes animal mess, the change of attitude is amazing: the chicken leaves small piles of poop all around the house. I am constantly picking up these smelly bits with a tissue but David is totally unconcerned. When our grand-children come to visit they are thrilled and spend hours playing with the 'house chicken'. It's very tame, and I start to wonder if it will ever be allowed to go outside and join the flock. I am also worried in case it turns out to be a rooster – this will mean, quite naturally, that it will end up in the pot. I don't think David will take kindly to eating his firstborn.

Eventually, when the bird has grown feathers to replace the yellow down, I convince David that it is mature enough to fend for itself in the big, wide world. We transfer the chicken to the fowl run and David takes over the feeding and egg-gathering completely. Cheepy Chicken is, fortunately, female and she runs to greet him every time he comes in to change the water and replace the layer pellets. They are the best of mates and, from my point of view, a very odd couple.

In my early to mid teens I agonised over my appearance, spending hours in front of the mirror lamenting my bright red frizzy hair and pasty white skin, and the brown freckles that, to my mind, totally disfigured my face and body. I hated my lack of breasts and my fatty thighs and really believed that I was too unsightly to attract any right-minded youth. In my later teens I discovered make-up and hair techniques to modify my looks slightly. I smothered my skin with a thick foundation to mask the freckles, wore upper and lower false eyelashes and spent hours straightening the kinks out of my hair by wrapping it around my head after washing it, using a scarf. I had many nights of uncomfortable sleep trying to keep this contraption in place. I suspect my teenage insecurity about my looks was no different from that suffered by many girls of the same age and, thankfully, by the time I hit my early twenties I had developed a comfortable, if not resigned, relationship with my face and body.

This casual acceptance of my physical appearance continued happily through my twenties and thirties and well into my forties. While my weight tended to fluctuate according to my lifestyle or whether I was pregnant or breastfeeding, overworked or relaxed, I was generally not too fussed about the way I looked when I had a moment to catch a look at myself in the mirror. Getting ready to go out took only a few minutes' preparation with a little eye make-up and some nail polish, and I allowed my hair to revert to its natural curl, which finally became a little more fashionable.

In my late forties I started to notice the first signs of physical decline. While I still felt as strong and physically fit as I had always done, I realised that my hair was starting to thin out on top and my eyes were surrounded by a patchwork of fine lines. A few wrinkles didn't cause me too much stress, but over the next five years the appearance of lines and cracks and crevices accelerated at an alarming rate. The aging process was most noticeable in photographs, especially close-ups, where the shadows caused by sagging flesh suddenly became profoundly apparent. Intellectually, I dismissed my concerns about the changing of my face as pure menopausal neurotics. I told myself that I didn't really care. All those expressions, once considered trite, suddenly applied to the way I felt.

'You should be proud of your wrinkles, you've earned them.'
'Your face has grown into itself.'
'The face of a mature woman has real character.'
'You get the face you deserve.'

To be quite honest, I preferred my face as it was before it acquired this newfound 'character'. And I didn't think I deserved what was happening to me in the mirror. Why did I 'deserve' that sag of flesh underneath my chin line, or those fine lines that were developing like a cat's bum around my mouth?

I suppose I should have felt resigned to my fate. After all, I had four adult children and seven grandchildren to testify to my 'mature' status in life. Yet somehow I felt cheated – as though I had worked like a mad woman my whole adult life only to be rewarded with a face that was rapidly falling apart. I'm not sure if this attitude is a baby-boomer thing, an overwhelming desire to defeat nature's clock and stay young no matter what. I would like to think that I'm immune to it, but I'm not.

Suddenly my cosmetics drawer is bursting with bottles and jars and tubes of creams and lotions with names like 'Visible Lift' and 'Age Defying All Day Lifting Foundation' and 'Skin Firming Lotion' and 'Total Turnaround Visible Skin Renewer' and 'Age-Intercepting Skincare', as if I really can turn this process round, defy my age and halt the process of gradual deterioration.

I know it's bunkum, but that doesn't stop me. A friend who for decades worked in the beauty business laughingly refers to these carefully marketed cosmetics as 'pots of hope', and that's exactly what they are. Expensive products aimed at the troubled minds of the women of my generation who are staring old age in the face and not enjoying the prospect.

One day in Bathurst I notice a beauty salon advertising 'non-surgical cosmetic procedures', which I assume means botox and collagen and all those associated treatments that promise wrinkle-dodging miracles. I make an appointment for a 'free consultation' to discuss the possibilities, in the belief that I am not taking any real action, just researching the subject for future reference. I am curious about what promises are being made and want to know if they believe any of these treatments are suitable for me. While I know that they will probably say just about anything to get a customer, I rationalise that I am savvy enough to make a decision based on fact rather than fiction.

The salon is located up a flight of stairs in an old, rather elegant building in a slightly out-of-the-way part of town. The lighting is subtle, the furnishings plush, and soft relaxation music is piped to every room – the sort of dolphin-worshipping/ incense-burning music I find so irritating. I am taken to a small private room with a massage table and invited to lie down and wait for the 'consultant'. She arrives, looking all of about twelve. She has flawless skin that has been creamed and polished to perfection. I am glad I can't see myself in the mirror to make a comparison.

We discuss the problems of aging skin and the benefits of various procedures, including facial massages and something alarming called 'dermabrasion', which involves 'resurfacing' the facial skin to reduce 'scars, pigmentation and congestions'. It sounds a bit like attacking my face with a sanding machine and I baulk at the prospect, knowing that my fair and sensitive complexion turns bright red if I sit in a hot bath for ten minutes. My young beautician then waxes lyrical about the possibility of a 'non-surgical facelift', involving an intensive facial and twenty minutes of laser therapy, which the brochure claims is 'ideal for the serious-minded facial client'. I am not sure if I fit this category.

Lastly, and with a little hesitation, I ask her about botox and collagen. This is when she becomes really excited.

'Botox is fantastic,' she gushes. 'The results are amazing.'

I ask if many women in Bathurst come in for these treatments.

'Oh, yes, lots of women have work done every three months,' she assures me. 'It's extremely popular out here in the country.'

I don't recall seeing many glamorous women swishing around.

the supermarket looking as if they have been freshly botoxed, but I take her word for it.

'I'm having botox myself in a few weeks,' she adds with conspiratorial delight.

I stare at her flawless young face, devoid of even a suggestion of a line or wrinkle.

'Why on earth would you do that?' I ask.

Immediately, she scrunches up her brows into an artificial frown. 'When I watch television I wrinkle up my forehead like this,' she says. 'My dad has a really wrinkled forehead and I know I am going to have the same thing. It's genetic. The botox is being used to stop me from frowning so I can never actually develop the lines. It's what they call a preventive treatment. I am really excited about having it done. I can't wait,' she adds with a beaming, smooth-faced smile.

I am horrified. The concept of injecting botox, which is 'a purified form of botulinum toxin Type A', into a youthful, line-free forehead seems decidedly bizarre to me, but I reserve my judgement.

I make an appointment for a facial the following week with one of the older and, I hope, more experienced consultants. On the advice of my young friend I am tentatively booked for 'dermabrasion' but I insist that I would like to discuss it further. It all sounds a bit drastic.

On my next visit I am taken to another private room and given a gown to change into. The beautician, an older and wiser woman, appears and examines my skin carefully. She comments on the red capillaries that are obvious just below the skin surface. I have always had these fine red veins that become apparent when I get hot. She confirms what I feel myself.

'Your skin is extremely sensitive and is certainly not suitable for anything like dermabrasion. In fact, even a facial massage is too invasive. It will just stir up all those fine red veins. A cooling treatment with moisturisers is all your skin type is suited to.'

I am glad to avoid the sandpaper; I'd have ended up looking like a lobster. But I am still curious about the botox. She tells me a Sydney doctor comes once every three months to do botox and collagen injections for local clients. I make an appointment.

David is horrified that I am even contemplating it, and I must say I am still less than convinced that it's a good idea. I rationalise that it's just my curiosity – and certainly the 'before' and 'after' photographs in the colour brochures do show a dramatic difference in facial appearance after treatment. For several months David and I have an ongoing debate on the botox issue; he doesn't soften even slightly in his vehement disapproval. So I decide to drop the subject and not tell him when I am going to see the 'cosmetic specialist'.

I am told to get to the beauty parlour at least half an hour before the appointment so that I can have 'anaesthetic cream' applied to the areas to be treated. I explain that I haven't finally decided to go ahead with treatment yet but would prefer to talk to the doctor first. However, they still want me to have the cream applied so I won't need to hang around longer than necessary should I decide to proceed.

Lying on the massage table, I am greeted by a smiling Louisa, who is the wife of Dr Paul, as he is called by all those working in the salon. 'Do you have any questions?' she beams.

'Yes, plenty.'

And I bombard the poor woman with questions about the

various treatments, how they work and possible side-effects. I mention that I loathe those 'Julia Roberts lips that look as if she has just been punched in the mouth'.

'You mean like mine?' she says, pouting. And I realise that that's exactly what her lips look like – swollen and distorted.

'Well, yes, now that you mention it. Did you have yours done with collagen?'

'Yes,' she replies with some pride. 'I just love this look, but you don't have to have it done like this. You can just have the fine lines on your upper lip smoothed out with tiny amounts of collagen. I had it injected into the body of the lip to change the shape. It's just a matter of personal choice.'

When I look closely I realise that Louisa is a walking advertisement for her husband's work. Every line and fold and crease, except for the very fine lines around her eyes, has been 'smoothed out', as the brochure says.

I shiver a little and wonder what I am doing here. Might be too late to back out now.

It turns out that I can't have collagen (phew) because I have to be given an allergy test for it first. A tiny quantity is to be injected into my arm to see if I have any allergic reaction. But I seem to be locked into having my forehead done. The numbing cream has taken full effect and it seems a bit churlish to back out now.

Dr Paul finally wanders in, all smiles and good humour. I talk to him briefly about botox, but he seems more concerned about the likelihood of pain. His wife prepares to hold my hand but I reassure them both.

'I've given birth without pain relief. I think I can manage this okay.'

Nevertheless, he further numbs my skin with blocks of ice and asks me to 'give him a big frown' so he can see where the lines are. This will guide him on where to insert the needle with the toxic bacterium that will paralyse the muscles between my eyebrows. I can't really believe I am doing this, but what the hell. I tell myself that I am just dipping my toe in to see what happens.

To distract me from any possible pain, I suspect, Dr Paul chats brightly during the few minutes it takes to botox my forehead. 'Men aren't very good at pain,' he says. 'I do my own botox in the mirror, but I have to stop all the time because I just can't stand it any more.'

The mental image of Dr Paul fainting in front of the mirror while botoxing his own wrinkled forehead appals but also delights me. It's just like that episode of 'Mr Bean' where Rowan Atkinson manages to paralyse the dentist, then proceeds to drill the holes in his own teeth in the mirror. It's almost impossible to watch such a grotesque performance.

I confess to Dr Paul that I haven't, as yet, told my husband what I am doing.

'I wouldn't worry about it,' he says dismissively. 'I'd estimate that 90 per cent of women who have work done never tell their husbands or boyfriends.'

'But, surely,' I protest, 'these men must notice a change in their wife's' appearance if, as you say, the treatments make an appreciable difference?'

He snorts. 'Men don't look at their wives.'

I am left wondering just who the women are doing it for. Themselves, I suppose. That must also include me. I am aware that David thinks it totally unnecessary. He has said so dozens of times. And I suspect that the man from Toulouse would also think it a rather pointless exercise. It's not as if I look a lot older than my years. Realistically, I look exactly what I am – a woman in her early fifties. It's just that I don't want to look like a woman in her early fifties. I want to look five or even ten years younger, and if I can achieve that with some relatively innocuous injections, then why not?

'All done,' he says. 'You were a model patient. If I had a jelly bean, I'd give you one.'

Bloody expensive jelly bean, is my only thought. $350 poorer plus $80 for the collagen allergy test. I ask the good doctor about the young girl in the salon who was planning a botox treatment, but he can't seem to recall having 'done' her.

'About the youngest patient we see is thirty,' he tells me, 'unless people are having it for genuine therapeutic reasons.'

I wander from the salon. There is no pain and the muscles between my eyes still work perfectly if I choose to frown. He says it will take two days to work and should last from four to six months.

Over the next few days I spend a lot of time looking at the small triangle of flesh between my eyes, wondering if there is any difference. Three days after the treatment I realise that I can't frown, even if I try. Frowning is an unconscious muscle movement and we rarely try to frown deliberately. Thus I don't walk around feeling numb or as though I have lost any facial sensation. However, when I look in the mirror and deliberately try to crease my brows by frowning, I can't. And the area looks smooth. So I suppose it has worked, but I wonder if it is worth it in terms of time, trouble and cost. Do I look any younger? I doubt it. But perhaps after the collagen in my lips . . .

25

For several years now I have been leading treks into remote regions of the Himalayas, taking groups of people to see alpine plants in their natural environ-ment. It's not so much a job as a passion, and I decide, now that I am no longer tied down by the television program, to take a few extra tours every year to the northern hemisphere. Jan and I have planned a detailed itinerary for an autumn walking-cum-eating and drinking tour of the region of France where we both live, and I have also agreed to take a tour group to northern France and southern England in the spring, to look at gardens and visit the Chelsea Flower Show – a highlight in any garden lover's calendar. This means leaving the farm unattended, because David has plans to visit the Cannes Film Festival, as he does most years. We have decided to meet up and spend time at the house in Frayssinet. It will be our first time there together and I am looking forward to it, even though the spectre of the man from Toulouse is looming.

Our son-in-law's father, John, has agreed to come and house-sit for seven weeks and take care of the animals. John has recently retired as an army captain and then music teacher, and has been travelling around Australia in a campervan on an extended sabbatical. He is looking forward to having a roof over his head for a couple of months, and being on the farm means that he is close to his four grandsons, whom he adores, and who adore him. Originally English, his preference is for a warm climate, and for the past eight years he has been living near Bundaberg, in Queensland. The shivering cold of the climate where we live will be a shock to his system, but we feel sure that he will cope. John is such a special character that I have written a children's story about him as a bit of fun for our mutual grandsons. The story is about John's uncanny knack of getting the children off to sleep by reading their bedtime stories in such a monotonous voice that they simply cannot keep their eyes open.

We run through all the practical things John will need to know about keeping the fires going, looking after the poultry and fixing the house pump if it should break down. David and I head off in different directions, leaving John and Floyd, our dog, standing at the top of the long driveway, waving. David flies to Nice en route to Cannes while I head off to Paris with half my tour group under my wing. The others will meet us when we get there.

People who go on gardening tours are usually earthy people with no pretensions and a great sense of fun. This group is no exception, although they hail from vastly different backgrounds, and when we all first get together I wonder how the chemistry of it will work out. I refer to this style of expedition as a 'twinset and pearls' tour, because it's all highly organised and comfortable. Air-conditioned buses, top-quality hotels, and excellent meals in the evening. A bit of a contrast to my adventure treks, where we sleep in tents and walk uphill for seven or eight hours a day. Women usually outnumber the men on both types of tour, exactly as they do in garden clubs, but on this tour I have two blokes to help balance the equation. Richard is a middle-aged man who is the 'travelling companion' of Margaret, an English-woman who runs an antique shop in the mountains. The other man is Colin, whom I have known for many years, a professional horticulturist with a string of award-winning gardens under his belt. He has never been on a plane before and his excitement at the prospect of visiting so many famous international gardens is palpable. There are other knowledgeable gardeners on this trip too – a young woman called Heather who operates a wholesale citrus nursery in a nearby country town, another Margaret, who owns one of the best garden centres in New South Wales, and several garden club members, including Pam, with beautiful gardens of their own. Then there's Debbie, nearly six foot tall and gorgeous with spiked blonde hair and a loud and very broad Australian accent. She's outrageous, and I wonder how she and the more quiet and conservative members of the group are going to get along.

Apart from anything else, it's my role to keep the travellers happy and harmonious – a bit like being the mother of a large family – and I sometimes wonder if I am just jumping back into that old familiar role again of looking after everybody else. There is a certain skill in making everyone feel good about the trip, especially people who come from different backgrounds and have different expectations of the experience. It's a bit of a juggling act, but I have had so much practice within my own family that keeping the atmosphere light and happy is second nature to me now. Whatever, I always have a lot of fun on these tours and bond so closely with some of the participants that we become friends for life.

We have several days in Paris, the primary purpose being to travel out to Normandy to see Monet's garden at Giverny. For some of the group this particular visit has been a lifelong dream, and even though we are all quite exhausted and jet-lagged when the bus picks us up for the two-hour journey, there is a great sense of excitement. The bus journey out of Paris is a little tedious and some of the group drop off to sleep, but once we get out into the countryside they cheer up as we drive through little villages and get a taste of French rural lifestyle. Monet's garden is one of the most visited gardens in the world, and bus groups are booked in at specific times so that there are not too many people in the garden at once. It's not a very large garden and it is divided into two distinct sections – the flower garden that adjoins the pink and green painted house and the water garden made famous by Monet's waterlily series of paintings.

Before we left Sydney airport, as we were walking to our boarding gate lounge we passed a Taronga Zoo shop selling lots of stuffed animals. Standing on the carpet outside the shop was a very large fluffy emu with wild eyes and a spiked head of hair like Debbie's. As we approached, one of the women said 'Look at that! Who would buy something as hideous as that?'

'I would,' I said reaching for my credit card. 'It will make a fabulous present for Jan, my friend who lives in the next village in France.' By the time we reach Paris, the emu, christened Flossie after the calf back home, has become our mascot on the tour – I carry it with us everywhere, even to Monet's garden.

The garden is financially subsidised by American art lovers and is always teeming with large groups of Americans who are mad about everything to do with Monet. The gift shop at the garden is enormous; it was once Monet's art studio, where he painted his massive waterlily canvases, but has been converted into a sophisticated money-making concern with Monet scarves, ties, teapots and books and the usual postcards and poster-sized prints of his paintings. I find it all a bit tacky, but I suppose it is essential to maintain the garden at such a very high standard. Several years ago an Australian artist whom I met at a garden club when I was showing colour photographic slides that I had taken of Monet's garden one late spring subsequently spent almost a year living in the village of Giverny, coming into the garden every day to paint. She told hilarious anecdotes about how when the gardens closed every afternoon at 4.30, the gardeners would scurry around like crazy deadheading the roses and tidying up for the following day. If a clump of a particular group of flowering perennials or bulbs, such as peonies or iris, started to fade, they would simply dig up the entire clump and bring in freshly flowering replacements from where they had been growing in a nearby field. It was sort of 'gardening by numbers', where everything was almost artificial in its perfection. I have always regarded the garden slightly differently since I heard this story, but for our tour groups it's two hours of sheer magic as we wander between the burgeoning flower beds and colourful borders.

Suddenly, a harsh female American accent pierces the air. 'Oh God, in Heaven's name, will you look at that? That woman's carrying a turkey under her arm!'

I affect a look of wounded outrage. 'It's certainly *not* a turkey, madam, it's a native Australian flightless bird. Have you never seen an emu?'

'It sure looks wild,' she says, giving Flossie a pat on her spiky head.

We take photographs of Flossie standing in Monet's garden, sniffing the roses, and from this moment the tour degenerates into a non-stop comedy routine, with Flossie as the centrepiece of our hilarity.

In Paris we catch the Metro to the splendid Jardin de Bagatelle in the Bois de Boulogne and spend a dreamy hot afternoon enjoying the thousands of roses that proliferate in this formal masterpiece. Margaret and Richard decide to snooze for a while beneath a shady tree but are moved on by the gendarmes, and Margaret is outraged at the thought of being treated 'like a derelict sleeping on a park bench'. On the way back in the Metro a young woman attempts to snatch her bag as we leave the station, a very common problem in Paris these days. I feel certain this young woman lived to regret this particular attempted theft. Margaret is so outraged that, clutching her bag tightly to her breast, she shrieks at the hapless and probably homeless figure: 'You wicked, wicked girl! How dare you try to take my bag? You wicked, wicked girl!'

The would-be thief takes off in terror and I joke that she is probably in need of counselling after this encounter. But we are all rather shaken, and from that moment become more aware of the dangers of big cities for tourists.

That evening Richard loses his wallet on the bus coming back from Montmartre. It's there one moment and gone the next. The poor chap spends his last day in Paris filing a report for the police and, while the wallet is turned in later in the day, the money and credit cards are gone. It takes the edge off our enjoyment of the day.

Some of us decide to see a live show while in Paris, heading off in the Metro to the outrageously expensive Moulin Rouge – it costs the equivalent of $180 for the show and a half-bottle of champagne. The standard of the show is fantastic, however, and I see how the can-can should really be done – a bit different from my frilly red knickers at the Yetholme Community Hall. One of the acts has me absolutely gobsmacked. A massive glass-sided water tank suddenly rises up from under the stage. It contains a very large python, at least four metres long, swimming under-water. A naked young woman appears and dives into the water, where she proceeds to 'dance' with the snake in a most lascivious fashion. I try not to laugh out loud, it's so over the top. A lot of the dancers at Moulin Rouge are Australians, I am later informed, chosen for their goods looks, long legs and athleticism.

The following day we take the train to London, where we will spend four nights before heading off on our tour of southern England. We arrive during the peak period of the Queen's Golden Jubilee and London is alive with shops selling tacky royal souvenirs and Union Jacks for those who wish to engage in a little flag-waving. As a dyed-in-the wool republican I am rather appalled at finding myself in London at such a time but some of the others are thrilled to be there during the celebrations. We enjoy some friendly banter about the pros and cons of the royal family and I buy some cheap and nasty souvenirs of the jubilee to hand out as prizes on the bus. I get a flashing plastic tiara for Margaret which she wears with great pride.

Debbie has taken to calling out that distinctive Australian bush cry 'COOOOOEEEEE' at the top of her lungs to gather the group together. She does it in the hotel foyer in the morning after breakfast and she does it when we are getting onto the bus.

Reserved English people passing by look at us with disdain, seeing a motley group of loud, noisy, Australian tourists (especially when they spy Flossie under my arm or staring out of the bus window with her beady eye). But we don't give a hoot; we are having a great time.

We do the Chelsea Flower Show and several famous public gardens in London, then pack up for our country tour, which will include the famous Sissinghurst Garden created by Vita Sackville-West. Our driver appears with the bus outside our smart Kensington Hotel. His name is Roy and he is alarming in appearance. Six foot seven inches (2 metres) tall, he weighs twenty-one stone (137kg) and has no front teeth. As he bends over to load our suitcases into the baggage compartment we are presented with a vision of him from the back – that fleshy cleavage revealed when a man's trousers or shorts don't quite cover the rear end. Some people call this spectacle 'builder's bum'. I try not to catch the eyes of the other women because I know we will dissolve into hysterics. Roy is just as alarming in behaviour as he is in appearance. He is charmed by Flossie but a little too familiar for some of our tour group's comfort. I am assigned the seat at the front of the bus, with a microphone, and I am also given a thick road map. It appears that I am expected to navigate because, once he leaves London, Roy doesn't have the vaguest idea where he is going. Every time I speak to the group or say anything at all, Roy's voice booms out in his marked London accent, 'Now, Mary, beeeeeeave yourself.'

He also has a habit of coming up behind me, and some of the other more friendly women in the group, and lifting me up in the air like a weightless rag doll. I quickly learn to see the look in the eyes of the other women as he approaches from behind and dodge out of the way. His favourite trick is to lift me up and bang my head – not hard – on the ceiling of the bus. While we are all amused at his antics, we also find him a bit odd, especially when he informs us that he has been married four times and two of his wives died in car accidents.

As we set off out of London, heading south, I start to wonder if Roy might have been driving when these accidents occurred to his wives. He is a truly terrifying driver. Not only does he drive far too fast for the road conditions, he steers the bus erratically, veering from side to side so that our hand luggage is constantly crashing from the overhead storage shelf and landing on our heads. It's impossible to stand up and walk down the aisle when Roy is driving, and after the first day I start telling him to slow down. I don't want members of the group to be nervous wrecks by the time we reach each garden.

This aspect of the tour is a nightmare. I have to tell him where to take each turnoff in the maze of road systems through rural England. As he tends to speed we are constantly overshooting the turnoffs and then finding ourselves trying to turn the huge bus round in a narrow country lane. He drives so quickly through the villages that we can't see and appreciate the architecture, and I seem to spend my entire day asking him to 'slow down' or 'take it easy'. The standard of the hotels where we are booked is excellent, but unfortunately not always up to Roy's expectations (he is staying with us for the entire tour). At one hotel they have allocated him a single room with a single bed and he digs in his heels. He's just too large, he explains, to fit into a single bed and they don't have another room available, except for a deluxe room with a massive four-poster. In the end the travel company agrees to pay the difference and Roy wallows in luxury – he had threatened to drive back to London and abandon us if he couldn't get a decent bed to sleep in. One night, Roy and I are given adjoining rooms and the porters bring our luggage up at the same time, knocking on each of our doors. We open them simultaneously and I find myself facing a half-naked Roy, only his trousers intact, with his massive bulk filling the entire doorway to his room.

''Ello, dangerous,' he says, leering at me.

I quickly grab my suitcase and slam the door, locking it immediately. I have decided that Roy is more of a liability than an asset, but we are stuck with him until the end of the tour. Might as well make the best of it.

The gardens, however, are gorgeous, the countryside lush and the small villages and towns are always interesting. We stay in Brighton and Bath and Stratford-on-Avon, where we see a Shakespeare performance in the evening. The group has bonded well and we have plenty of laughs along the way, trying to dodge Roy's clumsy advances and retaining our sense of good fun. We have a farewell dinner at a smart hotel in Bury St Edmunds; the theme is the Jubilee, and I ask everyone to dress up for the occasion. Fortunately, the hotel has allocated us a private room – some of the outfits are utterly outrageous, especially our professional gardener, who comes as a court jester complete with striped tights and codpiece. I wear high heels and fishnet stockings with a pair of Union Jack knickers that some of the group have bought me for a joke, a little reminiscent of my can-can outfit from home, but I am careful to remain well covered with a shawl between my bedroom and the private dining room. I don't think the hotel lobby is quite ready for this. However, late in the evening, after dinner and several bottles of Australian wine that we found at a local off-licence, our court jester decides to stand on his head in the foyer, causing a ripple of concern among the reception staff. We are quite certain they will be glad to see the back of us!

Back in London we take part in some authentic Jubilee celebrations, standing on a bridge over the Thames for the impressive jet flyover and then taking a dinner river cruise. One of our group is nearly refused entry because she is wearing joggers rather than 'feminine' shoes, but I manage to sweet-talk the maître d' who is being a bit of a stickler about the dress code. Once again, we have a hilarious night together.

I farewell my happy band of travellers in London and
head for France to meet up with David, who has been
at the house for several days, getting it ready for my
arrival. The flight out of London is cancelled at the last possible
moment – takeoff is aborted as we accelerate down the runway
and the plane is turned round and taken back to the terminal.
We are off-loaded unceremoniously and have to re-enter the
airport through Customs and wait around in the baggage area to
be told what alternative arrangements have been made for us. I
am aware that David will be anxiously waiting for me at Toulouse
airport and I only hope that the airline keeps those at the other
end well informed.

Unfortunately, my worst fears on this are realised. At Toulouse
a 'Cancelled' sign is simply displayed against my flight and
nobody at the information counter seems to know what is
happening. I have no way of contacting David and he has no
idea what has happened to me. Eventually, he tells me later, he
badgered a clerk at the Air France desk into calling London to

find out what had happened. The clerk doesn't have very good English, and when he comes off the phone he simply shrugs his shoulders and says 'engine failure'. David misinterprets this to mean some kind of accident and, by now frantic and distressed, dissolves into tears. Finally, from Heathrow, I manage to get a message through to Jock that I am catching another plane in a few hours, re-routed through Paris. David has been calling people in the village to explain why he is so late and, fortunately, at this point the news that I am okay finally gets through. I arrive in Toulouse seven hours behind schedule, dragging my luggage and a rather bedraggled Flossie, and we both acknowledge that it's not a very good start to our time together in Frayssinet. Indeed, it seems to be some kind of portent.

The next few weeks are not as blissful as we would have hoped. We have various visitors coming and going and, even though it's fun seeing friends and sharing our joy in our little village house with them, it's also quite stressful, and it means that we never really have any time to enjoy it on our own. And the underlying problem of the man from Toulouse is never very far from my mind. He knows that I am here with my husband and has not been in contact, but I am now feeling very nervous and unsure about meeting up with him when David eventually goes home, several weeks ahead of me.

Until now all my thoughts about this man have been idealistically romantic, but the reality of the situation has begun to impinge on the fantasy. What if I meet him and we sleep together and it's awful? I might have put myself and David through five months of agonising and heartache for something that could easily be less than wonderful. My relationship with David has become more passionate than it has been in years, and here I am about to betray his trust and go off with another man. Yet despite these doubts and fears I know that nothing can stop the momentum of the relationship at this stage. I have invested too much emotional energy to simply turn round now and say I've changed my mind.

Part of my agreement with David is that I should have some time alone at the house each year, so that I can write and cook and socialise and gradually start some renovations. But David is unsettled at the idea of my being here alone, for obvious reasons. Although he never voices his concerns, I can tell from his general demeanour that he is uneasy and not very happy about leaving. Who could blame him?

It's quite a different experience for me, being in France with my husband, when I look back on the long period when I was here on my own. All the friends I have made are my friends, relationships that I established as a 'single' woman, and it is difficult for David, who is not as gregarious as me, to assimilate and become part of the group. We also like to do different things. While David likes to go out and socialise from time to time, he's much more of a homebody and can't keep up the pace of my action-packed French social life. The endless round of lunches, dinners and drinks leaves him drained, while I thrive on it. He would rather jump in the car and go for a long drive with no particular destination in mind, just exploring and finding whatever is at the end of the road. I love doing that too, but it's hard to find time for days off with so much going on.

'I seem to be cramping your style,' he says when we are discussing the number of engagements I have pencilled into my diary for the forthcoming week. 'Can't we have a few quiet nights at home?'

Here's the rub. He is perfectly happy to stay home with me while I cook up something wonderful from the markets and we listen to music on the CD player (we still don't have television). I love that too, but somehow there are very few nights where it is possible unless I start refusing invitations. We have to compromise, and we do. We get away on our own quite a few times, have relaxing restaurant lunches and dinners and some much needed early nights.

David's nephew Andrew and his girlfriend Sue are on a bike-riding tour of France and they call in to stay for a couple of nights, which is great fun. In their thirties and full of energy, they love everything about this part of the country and we take them to markets and restaurants as well as cooking for them at home. The afternoon they set off south on their pushbikes after a simple lunch in our small kitchen, I decide to have a nap while David has a shower; our old hot-water service doesn't provide enough water for four showers in a row and he has been waiting several hours for it to heat up again. As I am lying on our bed reading a novel I hear roars of excitement and loud shouting coming from the direction of our local bar, Le Relais. I suddenly realise what all the excitement is about. It's the World Cup Final, and obviously the whole village has gathered in the bar to watch the contest on the big screen that Christian has put up for the football season. France was eliminated several weeks ago and the finalists are Germany and Brazil. I imagine, quite accurately, that the locals here will be barracking for Brazil: there's still a deep-seated anti-German feeling in this region, which was a stronghold of the Resistance.

I leap off the bed, apply some lipstick and call out to David in the shower, 'I'm off to the bar.'

'But it's only two o'clock,' he calls back. 'It's not nearly time for a drink yet.'

'It's the World Cup Final and I want to see how it's received over here. It's research, I'm looking for colour and atmosphere.'

I can hear David's sigh of resignation as I dash out the door. Bloody wowser.

Le Relais is packed to the rafters and I can barely squeeze through the crowd to the bar, where Christian pours me a beer. I recognise most of the locals, men mainly, but there are also a lot of strange faces and they are reacting to every move on the big screen by shouting and jumping up and down and waving their arms. It's pandemonium. There are four middle-aged men dressed in colourful kilts who are cheering loudly in perfect French – I find out much later that they are Scottish high school teachers, French teachers to be exact, who spend their annual school holidays in this region renting a gîte with their wives and children. Now I have no interest in football. I realise that this particular game is soccer (the ball is round) and, as one of our sons played soccer when he was eight or nine years old, I do have a vague idea about the rules. But I haven't been following the season so I have no idea about the players or the politics or the passions involved.

I eventually find a seat at a table with four strangers and, amid the din, I recognise their Irish accents. They are on holiday from Dublin and northern Ireland and they are downing beers and generally having a wow of a time.

'Who's winning?' I ask lamely.

'Nobody at this stage,' one of them replies. 'It's a draw.'

They are obviously keen for Brazil to get in front, and every time the ball nears the German goalposts there are loud roars and screams of approval. I never realised that watching a football game could be such a passionate and noisy experience.

Pascal is there to try to keep the drinks flowing, because surely this will be one of the biggest days of the year for the bar. But some people are sitting on their drinks, taking advantage of the great venue to watch the game but not doing what is rightly expected – swilling down enough drinks to make it worthwhile for Christian and his employees. So the four Irishmen and I try to balance the equation by drinking beer after beer – long after the game is over (Brazil won) we are still sitting in the bar laughing and talking and having a good time. They are staying at a nearby gîte with their families and have left their poor wives at home with the children while they are at the bar getting sozzled and enjoying the game. Eventually, David comes looking for me and I introduce him to my four new friends. We take them back to the house – they are interested in the cost and logistics of buying a house in France – and later that day we meet up with them again, this time with their wives and children, at the bar and restaurant by the lake, the Plan D'Eau.

'Typical of you,' says David later, but with no malice, 'to pick up four drunken Irishmen in the bar.'

It was fun, just the sort of spontaneous thing that I love doing but that causes David a little anxiety. He thinks I am going through my second childhood.

Living in a foreign land is always a challenge, and not simply because of the inevitable language and cultural differences. It's a question of feeling accepted, being part of the village in which you live, even if only for a few short months at a time. I often wonder, as I saunter down to the boulangerie for bread or to the Post Office to dispatch some mail, whether I will ever feel truly integrated into this village, no matter how friendly and welcoming the locals are. I am reminded that only a few decades ago people from one village to the next regarded each other as 'strangers' and would be upset at the notion of one of their children marrying 'out' by forming a liaison with someone from even ten kilometres away. Looking at the local phone directory, which lists residents and phone numbers village by village, it is obvious that people to this day have remained in their traditional areas, with large numbers of two or three family surnames in each village rather than spread out over a larger region. The names carved in stone on the memorial to the fourteen young people murdered by Germans in the village square in 1944 are still the surnames listed in the phone book, and they also mirror the surnames on the family vaults in the village cemetery. So while there has been a shift in population, with the younger generations moving to the cities to live and work, the family names still carry on, and I expect this will continue. Often, those who have lived and worked in the cities for thirty years eventually retire back to the village where they were born, and where their parents and grandparents probably always lived. It's hard for any outsider, especially one from a totally alien culture on the other side of the world, ever to become a real local under these circumstances.

For the French in the southwest, invasion by foreigners has been a way of life for more than a thousand years. The ongoing backwards and forwards by the English in particular in this region, formerly known as Aquitaine, is legendary, and to this day they maintain a strong presence, although now in a slightly different way – as local escapees from the awful English weather or as summer holiday-makers. They far outnumber the other foreign groups living full-time or part-time in The Dordogne and the Lot. The French have a funny acceptance of the English invaders, a sort of benign resignation to the fact that they will always somehow be lurking on the sidelines. The English, on the other hand, are simply using their common sense by rebelling against the ridiculous prices of houses in the United Kingdom compared with the comparatively cheap house prices in rural France. Not to mention the weather. Here in the south the sun shines much more frequently than in the United Kingdom; even when there is a summer storm a patch of blue eventually bursts through the clouds, and it's a rare day that doesn't include at least some cheerfully bright moments.

In many ways the English interlopers are the saviours of the provincial French economy, with an estimated thirteen million English visitors crossing the channel to France every year. The hard facts are that tourism accounts for 8 per cent of the French gross domestic product, and the main visitors are from England, Germany and Holland. The English and Dutch tend to spread out right across the country, whereas the Germans are more likely to congregate in a handful of places and mostly enjoy resort-style holidays rather than setting up permanent part-time holiday homes. The English also prefer to seek out places that are ignored by other tourists, which is why they can be found in remote villages in the poorer and less popular parts of the country. The conservative estimate of what the English spend in France annually is 5 billion euros (about $10 billion Australian).

The foreigners here fall into several categories. There are the slight misfits, who don't feel at home in their native land for some reason and have opted for a totally foreign alternative. Some are expats who have lived and worked in exotic locations most of their lives and can never really settle back into their home country. Jock, for example, originally from New Zealand, lived in Australia then New York for most of his working life; and Margaret Barwick, who with her husband David lived in tropical outposts on various diplomatic postings and then had no real 'home' to retire to, chose France for its relaxed appeal.

Some are genuine alternative lifestylers, like Bob and Carole, who fled hectic London in search of rural tranquillity; some are gay couples, both male and female, avoiding claustrophobic family contacts, perhaps; and some are elderly retirees who just prefer the cost of living in the French countryside. Some people are escaping from something back home, perhaps a failed marriage or a business that has gone sour, and France seems like a great place to start again. For some it's just the second-home option, a place to spend the summer that is more peaceful and secluded than overcrowded London in July and August.

There are lots of people like Jock, who love the cheap wine and excellent food, but there are also quite a few younger people with practical skills – plumbers and electricians and builders who find no trouble getting work because so many houses are in the process of renovation. Some of these tradespeople work 'black', which is a problem for those who are prepared to go through the bureaucratic nightmare of becoming legitimate residents with work permits, and declare their earnings and pay taxes. Those who work for cash in hand can underquote, and this causes jealousies and rivalries with the local tradespeople.

The final group of foreigners in France are the terminally boring, so frightful that their families have given them a one-way ticket in the hope of never seeing them again. These people can be difficult to avoid in social situations and are often loud and red-faced and scathing about the French. I suspect they would be critical of everything around them no matter where they lived; they are just a hazard of life in any community.

Foreigners who live in France either stick together socially or desperately try to avoid each other, preferring to mix with the local French population. A great deal depends on language skills. There are plenty of people who have lived in France for two decades or more and still have only rudimentary French, while others will make a heroic effort to gain fluency in order to establish and maintain relationships. At parties where English and French are mingling, inevitably the two groups drift apart as the evening wears on. Even the language-literate English who start out making an effort to converse all night in French become tired and lazy after a few glasses of wine and gravitate towards their English-speaking fellow party-goers. Things can get awkward when there is only one French person in the group – he or she is usually included in conversation in the early stages of the evening but left behind as the pendulum swings back to English.

In between dinner parties and lunches I spend a lot of time at my computer, sitting at the kitchen table looking out into the street. It's rather like being in a goldfish bowl, because everyone who passes by can see clearly into the room, but that doesn't worry me at all. At night, when the lamps are lit and I am sitting at the table sipping wine while the dinner cooks, it looks a charming scene from the street. Anne Rotherham says glancing in through the arched windows as you walk by is like looking into a scene from the film *Chocolat*. I wander across to the square and look for myself. Sure enough, the simplicity of the house is very appealing. I just love being in it, being part of the scene, with time to observe the comings and goings of my neighbours. Mme Thomas is interesting to observe. In her early seventies, I assume, she wears the typical blue floral cotton coverall that is the signature dress of every village woman of a certain age. She wears it with slippers as she neatly sweeps the front steps every morning and waters the pots of flowers, and wanders back and forth to the shops. She makes at least three or four trips past my front windows every day. First, she goes to the boulangerie to get her bread for lunch. She wanders past and waves, giving me a friendly smile. Twenty minutes later and she's off again, this time to the alimentation. She buys a few bits and pieces, probably cheese and cream or milk, but not vegetables or fruit because she and her husband grow their own. She probably also buys the local newspaper, then saunters back up the hill to her house. An hour later and she's on the road yet again, this time to the Post Office. More waves, more smiles. Her last trip is to the charcuterie to get something to cook for her husband's lunch. I have been into her kitchen in the late morning and the room was filled with the fragrance of a rich stew she had obviously been slow-cooking from the day before. All this coming and going obviously helps to fill up her morning and must also keep her quite fit. She's slim enough and looks as healthy as can be. She disappears in the afternoons – having a nap after a glass of wine, I suppose – then spends the late afternoon pottering in her garden. Not a bad life, not a bad life at all.

While David is staying in Frayssinet, I manage to also catch up with the friends I made during my first long stay in France. Lucienne continues to play hostess at various dinner parties, and her cooking skills never fail to impress me. There are never fewer than five courses and the meals are always well balanced – with a mixture of light and heavy courses that are much easier to cope with than the usual course after course of rich and heavy ingredients. Lucienne also knows her wines very well, and we can be assured of tasting some really good vintages whenever we are at her table.

I also catch up with Pam, a retired English actress who has been very kind to David during the two periods he has been in France without me. I guess it's their mutual interest in show business and music that draws them together and I am relieved that there is one strong connection he has made without me being around. David has also established a great rapport with

Margaret Barwick, whose weighty reference book on tropical trees is very close to being published. It's funny for me to meet another gardening writer living and working on the other side of the world, and especially amusing because our areas of knowledge and expertise are so different. Here I am coming from Australia, where there are vast areas of tropical flora, and I'm totally fascinated by alpine plants from the northern hemisphere. And here is Margaret, living and writing in cold old southwest France with an abiding love of all plants tropical. She did spend decades living in the tropics, but the irony of our different interests is certainly not lost on me.

I have also been planning an overnight trip to Lourdes with my English friend Anthony, who is still beavering away renovating his old farmhouse in a nearby commune. I have always wanted to see Lourdes, more from amused curiosity than a desire to be cured by the magical waters, and Anthony is happy to do the driving because he is also a little intrigued by the lure of this highly commercialised holy site. Anthony seems to be taking forever to restore his old stone house and he spends his life cramped into one of the small barns with his collection of high-tech computers and electronic gizmos. This season he has made one giant leap forward, installing a large swimming pool on the edge of his land, overlooking a lush and tranquil valley. But while the swimming pool is quite opulent his own living quarters are terribly small – he has to climb over boxes of crockery and glasses to get to the fridge if he is fetching us a beer. His only seating inside is a floral plastic garden swing with a canopy, which looks hilarious juxtaposed with his whizzbang computer collection. The large farmhouse has been completely gutted and everything internal has been replaced: walls, floors and beams. It's a massive undertaking and progress seems slow from an outsider's perspective. We are all anxious for him to get in a kitchen and a bathroom and some central heating so he can get out of the pokey barn and be comfortable. But I think he secretly enjoys his monk-like existence.

Our planned Lourdes trip does not eventuate because Anthony injures his back lifting heavy beams and doesn't feel up to the long, possibly bumpy drive. We agree that it will definitely be on our agenda next visit.

My other English friend, Danny, whose partner Sue died tragically two years ago from a sudden cerebral haemorrhage, is looking a lot better this year and has found some happiness with a new woman in his life. Although she lives and works full-time in Britain, Christine is able to come over to visit Danny a couple of times a year and has endeared herself to all of the people in our circle of friends.

Roger the artist, who first introduced me to the delights of mushroom hunting in the woods, is just as reclusive as ever. It's difficult to lure Roger out for social events, although he did come to our curry birthday party. Roger has excellent dinner parties – he's an accomplished cook – and prefers to meet with people on his own territory rather than around restaurant tables or in the bar. He's probably a lot wiser than the rest of us.

Miles and Anne, who grappled with the pine marten problem in the spring, have arrived down from London in a shiny Porsche which has caused quite a titter of amusement in the community. Flash cars aren't the norm here in rural France, but Miles sees himself dashing around the country lanes at high speed. His wife and daughter see the Porsche as a form of mid-life crisis. Indeed, his daughter tried to discourage him from buying it in the first place, telling him he'd just look just like a silly old git with grey hair driving a sportscar.

Which he does, of course. But he is not discouraged and roars through the village, causing the locals to lift their heads out of their pastis, momentarily, and stare.

Miles and Anne have a beautiful wild sort of French rural garden and they also grow vegetables – potatoes and asparagus in particular – which they harvest during their annual long holiday in Frayssinet. This year they also decide to try bee-keeping – or at least Miles decides after talking at length to Philippe, who also keeps bees, over a very long and wine-soaked lunch one summer afternoon. Within a day a hive has been installed in their garden and Philippe has even tracked down a swarm of bees and introduced them to their new home. It all seems rather crazy, keeping bees when you live in another country, but part of the appeal of holidaying in France is getting into some of the local culture. Sadly the bees died during the following winter and the whole project had to be restarted. Practicality obviously isn't always a priority.

Although my book *Au Revoir* has only been out for five months it has already created a few waves in the villages around Frayssinet. The locals who speak only French haven't read it, of course, but they are aware of its existence and highly amused that their little corner of the world is being read about in faraway Australia. At Mme Murat's rustic restaurant, several couples have come in clutching a copy of the book and asking if this is indeed the restaurant that I have described in such detail. Jeanne Murat, who still runs the restaurant like a tight ship, and her beautiful daughter Sylvie, who is the glue that holds it all together, are thrilled when these curious Australians arrive, and serve them their five-course lunch with extra care. Sometimes, they are even asked to sign the book, which pleases them. When I come in for lunch the first time on this visit, Sylvie and Jeanne give me big hugs and plenty of kisses, plus a complimentary glass of sparkling wine. It makes me feel very special and appreciated.

Hortense, who runs the alimentation across the road from our house, is also accosted by Australians who ask, 'Which is Mary's place?'. When it's pointed out, they take photos. This sends a slight shudder down my spine, reminding me of my reasons for fleeing Leura, but at least it happens only once or twice. St Caprais, where Jock lives, also has a few visitations. Jock's house is signposted with a wooden shingle saying 'Jock's Trap' so he's easy to find even among the labyrinth of old stone dwellings. One couple actually knock on the door and introduce themselves to Jock; they turn out to be interesting people who part-own a French house nearby. Jock asks them in for a drink, naturally, and we all end up going out to lunch together. It's a rather riotous afternoon and I am sure we will see them again if we happen to be in France at the same time.

Jock also gets a phone call from a young woman on a semiworking overseas holiday. She has read my book and tracked him down through a mutual contact, a journalist who once worked with Jock. She would love to meet us both, so when she turns up we all get together for a drink and lunch at Mme Murat's. Her name is Vivienne and she is a photographer. She brings her camera to the restaurant, where we meet up with Harriet, Danny, Christine and Anthony. Jeanne Murat's father, known as Pépé (Grandad) still lives in a room over the restaurant and is well into his nineties. We decide to get some photographs with him – he's such an old character with his black beret and toothless grin – and Vivienne and Danny take charge of the cameras. While I am posing with my arm around Pépé's shoulder he starts squeezing my bum, then patting it. Some Frenchmen never give up the game, it seems.

In late June David and I both have our birthdays and we decide to throw a party in the house to repay some of the hospitality extended to us by our local friends. I decide to cook up a variety of curries, but finding the spices and condiments in France isn't always easy. The markets do have a beautifully presented herb and spice stall with baskets brimming with the most richly coloured array of powdered and ground ingredients from all around the world. But the way that they are displayed – out in the open day after day – means that in many instances they have lost the intensity of their flavours. Our neighbour Claude comes to the rescue. Every time he travels to Britain, which is at least twice a year, he buys small packets of herbs and spices from Asian stores in London and brings them back to Frayssinet, where he stores them in sealed containers in the dark, the only way to retain their flavours. I dig into his reserves of turmeric and garam marsala and cumin and fenugreek and put together a range of curries that have real depth of flavour. It's quite tricky cooking up a feast for thirty people in our inadequate kitchen. The stove is okay, but I don't have many large dishes or enough pots and pans for such a feast, so again I raid Claude's wonderfully equipped kitchen and come away with copper pots and serving platters and wooden plates that are ideal for serving curry. It's a hot day; both parties I have given in France have been on blazing hot days, and our house is small and overcrowded. But we have a courtyard and I set up tables and chairs outside and we have an enjoyable afternoon together. My main worry is the floor in the back half of the downstairs room, which is of crumbling chipboard tacked over dodgy beams. It creaks and sags every time it's walked on and I hope it will stand up to the weight of thirty enthusiastic curry eaters. It does, but we realise that this will have to be our first major expense: ripping up the floor covering and putting down new boards.

We get a call from John in Australia to say that all is fine at the farm, although there have been a few minor hiccups. It's been cold, very cold indeed, with overnight temperatures of minus six and minus eight, and most of his time and energy have gone into keeping the two main fires going all day and night. Our massive woodpile, which we hoped would last for several winter seasons, is gradually disappearing – he hopes there will be some left by the time we come home. Disposing of the ashes has been a bit of a problem for him. I normally chuck them in the compost or around various parts of the garden but John has been wrapping them up and putting them in the huge hessian wool bale where we put our rubbish for collection by a local contractor once a month. One morning he comes out to find that the entire wool bale has vanished overnight, complete with rubbish, with only a few burnt-out catfood cans left as evidence of the overnight conflagration. It's fortunate that the entire shed hasn't burnt to the ground, because it contains three cars, several large drums of oil and fuel and all the remaining wood supply.

John has also been having an ongoing battle with Laurie, who tries to corner him every time he goes into the pen to gather eggs and replenish the grain supply. John won't venture near Laurie unless he's carrying a large stick to fend Laurie off. The most dramatic incident that has occurred, however, involved old Floyd, who is half-blind. It seems that one afternoon a very attractive Husky bitch called Gemma, who was in season, sidled up the long drive and had her way with Floyd despite his age and arthritic joints. The problem was that they became enjoined, or 'stuck', as breeders sometimes call it, and John simply didn't know what to do. In his panic he eventually hosed them down, despite the freezing conditions, and finally they managed to separate. It turned out the Husky was owned by some new neighbours, a young couple who have built a cottage across the road, and they weren't aware that she had escaped. We wonder if anything will come of the union. If it does, I guess they will be Huskadors.

In the meantime I am busy firming up all the last-minute preparations for the September walking tour. Jan and I visit all the hotels and confirm the bookings and have lengthy discussions with the bus company, finalising the logistics of the itinerary, hoping that our French bus driver will be a little more refined and professional than Roy. Soon it is early July, and David leaves for Australia.

28

 I finally pluck up the courage to take the train to Toulouse. We have agreed by phone to meet on a street corner and, because our meeting time is mid-morning, we will go directly to a hotel room rather than out to a restaurant for lunch. In a way both of us need to confront this thing once and for all, without hours of seductive foreplay, sipping wine and talking. It has reached a stage where it needs to be dealt with in the stone-cold sober light of day.

Entering into a sexual relationship with a new person after so many years is a little daunting. I have often wondered how widows and divorcees handle going out 'on a date' with someone for the first time after a long-term marriage has ended. For many it must be such a terrifying prospect that they simply don't bother, and who could blame them? It's like starting all over again, but without the benefit of youth, innocence and firm flesh.

For me, the major surprise is that making love to another man seems the most natural and easy thing in the world. I feel comfortable and at ease with myself, as if the whole encounter is somehow right. I had never even kissed another man on the lips during all those decades, but when I kiss my lover for the first time I am not even vaguely unnerved. It feels perfect.

During the seven months preceding this relationship I have been unsettled by the thought of allowing another person to see me naked, especially as my body at fifty-two bears little resemblance to my body at twenty-one, when I first began my relationship with David. Yet, surprisingly, even that moment is easy. I am not even vaguely self-conscious or awkward. I am, instead, enraptured by the entire experience.

The only explanation I can give for the ease with which I cross this threshold is that I already feel very close to and familiar with the man from Toulouse by the time we finally embark on the physical part of our relationship. I am sure that if he had made a clumsy pass at me when we last saw each other, I would have rebuffed him on the spot. Yet because the closeness has developed gradually over the telephone and via email, the actual moment of our getting together has been so well anticipated that there is no risk of either of us being startled or taking flight. I have read a lot about Internet romances yet this is quite a bit different. I have already met this man and our mutual attraction has been established. It's just that our relationship has evolved, and here I am in a French city with my lover, having planned and plotted our affair from opposite sides of the planet.

Our love affair is brief and intense. Our meetings have to fit around his work and home life and my busy lifestyle. I am trying to avoid making David suspicious so I need to limit my trips to Toulouse and to be back in Frayssinet at times when he will be phoning from Australia to see how I am. It becomes an elaborate web of deception, but for me the stolen moments make it all worthwhile.

After I get off the train we meet in a bar and have a quiet drink, then he takes me to a restaurant of his choosing. He knows Toulouse intimately and I sense that he is making an effort to create a heightened romantic atmosphere around our meetings. He doesn't try to impress me by choosing particularly expensive or upmarket restaurants. Instead, he takes me to places that I would never discover myself as a foreign tourist, out-of-the-way places known only to a few locals. He invariably takes charge, ordering both our meals from the menu, because he knows the speciality of each establishment.

He leans towards me and says, 'I think you will like this dish. They have been doing it here for many years and they do it absolutely perfectly.'

He orders the wine with great care, discussing his choice with the wine waiter in almost conspiratorial fashion, as though they are plotting together to create the perfect dining experience.

Not for a moment do I feel as though I am surrendering my independence by just allowing all this to happen, just to unfold. And I find it hard to describe how much I enjoy the sensation of being led by the hand into unfamiliar territory. It is like being allowed for a few brief moments into another world, like dipping my toe into a culture and lifestyle that I have only ever read about. Yet here I am, sitting very close to my lover in the corner of a restaurant. He touches me often, touches my hand or my cheek or my knee, and we talk and laugh and share a level of intimacy that I find exciting but also a little disturbing. While we are both anticipating our inevitable move from the restaurant to the hotel he has booked, it's the enjoyment of our conversation that really surprises me. I somehow thought it would be just about sex, but it isn't like that all. It's the whole experience – the meeting, the atmosphere of the places we go to together, the easy banter between us. Part of me knows that it isn't real – this isn't what everyday relationships are based upon – yet part of me relishes every detail of the unreality. It's all a dream, a fantasy, except that it is actually happening and it's happening to me.

The man from Toulouse is amazed that I have never had an affair before. When I ask him about his own sexual history with women other than his wife, he smiles enigmatically. Of course he has had affairs, not that many, but a few over the years. I wonder if I am just naive, playing into the hands of a serial womaniser. Or if I am fortunate to have fallen into a relationship with a man who has the experience to make this brief dalliance even more exciting.

One aspect of our relationship fascinates me. The man from Toulouse treats me as I have never been treated before. He is thoughtful and courteous in a way that I can only describe as old-fashioned. As a liberated woman of the Sixties, I am astounded at the way in which our affair is conducted. He always designates a meeting place and is waiting for me when I arrive. I never have to wait even a moment for him. He is there, smiling and welcoming. He takes care of all the logistics with the minimum of fuss. Accounts are paid and taxis are ordered and I am barely aware of it. When the time comes for me to leave, to catch the train from Toulouse back home, he takes me to the station in a taxi and makes sure I am safely where I need to be. His attitude is both solicitous and protective and I find it most appealing.

Tingling from head to toe, I sit on the train in the late afternoon, on the way back to Cahors, wondering if it is all a dream. Can this really be *me* having an affair? It's not the sort of thing I do. I have never even contemplated it. Yet here I am swept up in the intensity of a new relationship and loving every moment of it.

As the time grows near for me to leave France and
return to Australia I have several earnest conversations
with the man from Toulouse about our painful
situation. We both know that the time is fast approaching for us
to reach some resolution about our relationship but we put it
off until the last possible moment – until our last day together,
our last lunch.

Guilt has never entered into my feelings about what has
happened. I don't feel guilty about his wife or my husband,
although I do feel extremely nervous at the prospect of either of
them discovering the affair. What worries me is the inevitable
distress that such a revelation would cause, not just to our respective spouses but to our wider families – to our children in
particular.

From the outset we both felt strongly that we were not entering
into this relationship as a way of escaping from our marriages.
He is very much a family man with a strong sense of his own
identity and his place in the world. Likewise, my commitment to

my family is unshakable, and I also feel very much an Australian woman in every sense. While I love France and want to spend part of each year living there, I certainly can't imagine abandoning my husband and my home, my family and my country to take up a new relationship on the other side of the world.

For us both there has been a clear understanding from the start of what this was to be – an affair, nothing more. An interlude of heart and mind, a brief encounter. Not permanent, not damaging or negative.

Of course nothing is ever that simple. You can't take a relationship and define it in such limiting terms. You can't use terminology to categorise what passes between a man and a woman, because it has to do with feelings and chemistry, reactions and emotions. The truth is that the 'affair' is more heartfelt than either of us anticipated when we first recklessly embarked on it. We care more for each other than we ever intended and so keeping a lid on the situation is extremely difficult. I want to be cool about it, matter-of-fact and casual. So does he. I don't want to phone him when we are apart and he doesn't want to phone me. But we do. It is an irresistible attraction, a sort of madness that feels as if it will never go away. Intellectually, we are in total agreement about what the future holds for us – absolutely nothing. Yet we both feel shattered.

Nevertheless we end it. We say 'no more' and terminate the relationship. I pack my bags, hand my house keys to Jan and with a heavy heart catch the train from Gourdon to Paris to connect with my homeward flight to David in Australia. At the airport I bolster myself with several strong gins – not a good choice, as it is famous for causing melancholy. Sitting in the bar, feeling lost and strangely disembodied, I very nearly miss the plane because I am so engrossed in my own sad feelings. After take-off I have another drink and swallow a sleeping pill. I tend not to sleep well on planes but, remarkably, I fall into a deep coma that lasts more than eight hours. Nervous and emotional exhaustion (not to mention alcohol and pills) totally wipes me out yet, when I wake up, having missed both dinner and breakfast, I feel curiously light and happy. I can't understand why I feel so good, but my sadness has lifted and I am left with a sense of relief that the tension is finally over. Even though the relationship lasted only for a few short weeks, I must have been coiled up like a spring for the entire time. Now that it has ended I come back to earth and feel grounded and focused.

I am left with a smug, joyful sensation. I can't believe I've really had this experience. My brain skips through all the special moments with the man from Toulouse and, instead of feeling devastated that it has finished, I am thrilled with the memory of it. I have managed to get away with something remarkable, without hurting anyone in the process.

When David picks me up from Bathurst airport he appears relieved to see me and I am thrilled to throw my arms around him. I have just walked away from the most unsettling experience of my life and I feel so drained that having the arms of my large, familiar and loving husband wrapped around me is the most unexpected but enormous relief. It is cold and wintry as we drive back to the farm, where I am greeted by the warmth and love of my big, noisy family. All the fires are alight, the vases are overflowing with flowers and the house is filled with the aromas of Sunday lunch cooking. I am home. I am safe. I am happy. I give all the grandchildren their presents and empty my purse of my French loose change, which our oldest grandson, Eamonn, collects with great care. He doesn't just throw the coins and notes in a jar, he catalogues them according to the date they were minted and their denomination, then works out their value in Australian dollars. I hope he won't end up a merchant banker, though he has the sort of personality that might be suited to it.

After lunch we go for a walk around the farm then sit about in front of the fire, drinking wine and catching up on the news from Bathurst and France. It appears that Gemma, the tarty Husky from across the road, is indeed in pup and that Floyd will be a father in four or five weeks' time. Miriam is keen to have one of the pups, especially if there is a female. John barely survived the winter temperatures at Yetholme and drove north at high speed the day after David arrived back to take over the reins of the farm. There's very little wood left in the shed and Aaron and Ethan have spent the last few weekends trying to collect another decent stack to get us through the winter. I catch up on news of our grandchildren but, as the afternoon wears on, I feel jet-lag creeping over me. The families pack up and go home, to Bathurst, Mudgee and Wentworth Falls. David and I sit by the fire and I struggle to stay awake, trying to last until nightfall so as to get back into a normal sleeping pattern.

He sits quietly opposite me on the sofa. 'I know about the man from Toulouse,' he says.

Speechless, I simply burst into tears. The game is over.

'It's all right, I understand,' he says, much to my amazement.

David is much more astute than I have given him credit for.

Ever since I first hinted, all those months ago, that I was feeling an attachment to the man from Toulouse, he has been tuned into my moods and emotions, and knowing me as well as he does, it's been perfectly obvious that I was heading towards an affair. I had also sent out lots of signals during the period leading up to my return to France and when we were together at the village house in the middle of the year. The most obvious signal had been in a newspaper interview I did after the release of *Au Revoir*. I was asked by the journalist what I would do if I knew I had only one more year to live. I nominated a 'wish list' of unfulfilled dreams that included taking my grandchildren on a trip to France and taking my own four children trekking in the Himalayas. My final wish was to have a love affair, then come home to David and die quietly, sitting on the front verandah with a glass of wine in my hand. For David it has been as though I have been waving a huge banner in front of his face, announcing my intentions.

How should a husband react when he knows that his wife of thirty-one years has just had an affair? I would have thought with rage, possibly bitterness and even revenge. However, this is not what happens.

While David is far from happy, he is not angry. He doesn't raise his voice, although he is quite obviously very upset and hurt. What he says to me is that he feels sympathetic to my pain and takes much of the responsibility for what has happened on his own shoulders.

The fact that our relationship has become stale over the past few years and that I am obviously carrying around resentment for various perceived failures on his part – some dating back more than twenty years – is the reason, in his mind, that this situation has occurred.

Confirmation came in the form of our phone bills, which indicated that I had been making regular calls to France for more than six months. These days every number is itemised and there were dozens where I had phoned Toulouse to say the coast was clear, then hung up so that my friend could call me back. David had also, just once, picked up a phone extension when I was talking to France. He assures me he didn't listen to the conversation, but in the few brief moments he was there he sensed the intimacy between us. It was enough for him to put two and two together.

'Why didn't you say something about it when we were in France?' I ask.

'I don't know,' he says, suddenly looking devastated. 'I just felt it was all out of my control and I thought confronting it there and then might make matters worse. It obviously just had to run its course.'

What is causing David the most pain is not the fact that I had a sexual relationship with the man from Toulouse, but that I had fallen in love with him. Several times David tells me that he would much rather I'd just had sex with someone I had met in a bar. He refers to an incident I wrote about in *Au Revoir*, when a bicycle rider tried to pick me up in the hotel in Villefranche-du-Perigord and I ran away. From David's perspective it would have been preferable for me to indulge in a couple of one-night stands rather than give myself heart and soul to another man. But he knows that I am just not capable of casual sex; my inevitable emotional involvement is much more threatening and dangerous.

The next few weeks are a roller-coaster of emotions. Within days the entire family knows and the phones are running hot with family members trying to come to terms with what has happened. Although not at all approving, Miriam is easily the most understanding of our children and takes on the unenviable role of counsellor, listening first to her father for hours, then hearing my side of the story. Knowing how busy she is with her large family I try not to weigh her down with the responsibility of being the 'go-between', but she naturally takes that position. When she thinks either of us is being overemotional or unreasonable she tells us. Without ever taking sides she somehow negotiates the difficult territory between her parents. We are not at war but there are so many issues to talk through. The affair has brought everything to a head and it has to be sorted out now or we risk falling apart.

Our sons are less forgiving. After the initial shock – and they are genuinely shocked – they phone me individually and voice their opinions. While I should be pleased that our family works in such an open, honest way and that they are quite comfortable letting me know exactly how the situation has affected them, I am also shattered by some of the things they say to me. They are disappointed. They feel let down. They feel that I have betrayed the sense of values that I instilled in them as children. They are worried, indeed angered by the pain I have caused their father. They are deeply passionate about what has happened and I am surprised at their intensity. I realise that for the entire time I was contemplating the affair, and certainly while it was happening, I didn't for a moment consider how my children might feel about it. Now it's out in the open and I am having to wear their anger and disapproval.

I feel swept along as if in a dream. I am powerless to do very much to resolve the situation, except to keep the dialogue between us open. I feel that if we can just keep talking about it, eventually there will be some sort of resolution. For the first time I am incapable of making everything all right again for everyone. There is a major emotional storm engulfing my entire family and I am the creator of it.

Trying to explain to our children how the situation evolved, I am careful never to try to justify my actions. I don't feel, for one moment, that I need to. I am also quite adamant that I feel no guilt or remorse. I try to explain to them that the affair itself was a good experience for me and one that I shall never regret even though I know it has caused a lot of pain. But eventually I get angry and defensive. And it is David who must bear the brunt of this reaction.

'Why is everyone so bloody upset?' I shout at him. 'I didn't do anything all that wrong. I had an affair, that's all. I didn't murder anyone. I came home, didn't I? It's over and done with. Can't we all just get over it, and move on?'

It takes a while, but eventually we all do, even David. We have some terrible moments, but we also have some moments of pure joy as we go through the process of talking it out and coming to terms with it and laying it, finally, to rest. At times we are even able to laugh about it. And what surprises me more than anything else is that my sexual feelings for my husband are stronger than they have been for many years. And his for me. I have read that having an affair can be good for a marriage, and in that respect it certainly seems to be good for ours. But in the overall scheme of things it really isn't, I finally conclude, such a wonderful idea. While it was thrilling for me and for the man from Toulouse when it was actually happening, it was extremely painful for us both to let go of each other at the end. It has caused pain to a large number of people I love and whose love and respect are very important to me. And it has changed my marriage forever. In many respects I love David even more for his tolerance and forbearance in the face of my betrayal, but for him something has vanished from our relationship that can never be restored.

I am due to remain in Australia for six weeks before returning to France to lead the walking tour that has been twelve months in the planning. For David this is the really difficult part. Having been through so much and gained so much in terms of the intimacy of our 'new' relationship, I am about to head off again back to France. However, I don't share his feelings. Not only am I going to France I am also going to Canada in late September to finally meet my sister Margaret, and the prospect of this far outweighs any nervousness about being back near Toulouse and all the emotion that it brings up. Margaret and I have been writing to each other for months now, gradually filling in the gaps and exchanging photographs and family information and we have decided that the time is right for us to meet, after a separation of fifty years. My brother Jon – her full brother and my half-brother – has been in contact with her too, and he is planning to visit her in August on his way to France. They haven't seen each other for fifty years either – he was twenty and she was nineteen when they last saw each other – and I am happy at the prospect of their reunion. I am also pleased that Jon is going to spend some time in our French house. He hasn't travelled overseas for more than thirty years, and it's only the desire to see his sister that has spurred him to make this journey. After Canada, I am heading to Nepal to lead a Himalayan trek, and David is far from happy about this, too, because of the political unrest in Nepal. But, as usual, I'm ready to leap in with great enthusiasm. I feel certain that trekking in the mountains will help restore my sense of who I really am, and enable me to put recent events further into the past.

Until it's time to go, life on the farm drifts along quite happily and for the first time I start to feel that this place is really 'home'.

Gemma from across the road has six beautiful pups, three males and three females, an attractive mix-and-match of the two breeds. When the young owner brings them across in a basket for us to admire, Floyd lifts his leg and piddles on them, which I don't regard as a particularly loving fatherly gesture. Miriam has chosen a female pup and we weaken and also select one. It will be a good guide dog companion for Floyd when he eventually loses the sight in his other eye.

We have a major disaster on the poultry front. The chicken house is raided one night and I discover corpses everywhere the following morning. The hit list includes one of the two remaining female muscovies, David's much loved Cheepy Chicken, two excellent laying hens and our handsome brown and white rooster. We suspect it's local dogs rather than a fox. Foxes take one bird at a time and rarely leave behind much more than a feather. This invasion was a total massacre, with ducks lying dead near the pond and chicken remains scattered across the paddock, leading to another farm. For some reason, that horror of a drake, Laurie, has escaped unscathed.

I will be leaving David in charge of all the poultry; the weather is still quite cold and bleak even though it is meant to be early spring. I will be gone for nine weeks and he is not looking forward to it. I know it will be difficult for him being alone again, and I hope he doesn't spend the time stewing on what has happened. He has become much more positive and energetic since he resumed his exercise regime, and I am hoping that this improvement in his frame of mind will counteract the reservations he has about his wife gallivanting around the globe.

I have organised to get to Frayssinet a week ahead of the tour to finalise the last-minute details. Jon is there to meet me at the station, although he is leaving to return to Australia the following morning. We couldn't quite coordinate things so that we could spend more time here together. Jon has had the most fantastic three weeks in France, making many friends and doing a lot of sightseeing. He has also done some painting for me – the front door and windows are now a soft shade of apple green – and some work on the car. I am grateful for his practicality.

Jan and I are looking forward to the tour, hoping we don't make any of the same blunders we made when we originally walked our way through the itinerary. Jan is ideal for this job. She's blonde and bright and bubbly and people instantly warm to her enthusiasm and good humour. She's also a bit wicked, like me, and when we get together anything can happen. The Australian travel agent who is organising the logistics of the tour, Paul, is coming along on this, the first of what we hope will be many tours, to help out and see how it all fits together. He also enjoys a bit of fun, so we hope our tour group is good-natured and easygoing.

The people in the group are arriving en masse at Toulouse airport and Pierre, the bus driver, will pick them up and bring them to their hotel in Cahors. Jan collects me in the late afternoon and says, as we walk to the car, 'As I was leaving the house there was a funny little squeak and I looked around. It was Flossie. She wants to come on the tour as well.'

Oh God, another epic journey with a demented emu. I'm sure they'll love her.

The people on the tour group turn out to be a great bunch, hell-bent on having a good time. Once again, they are mostly female, apart from Paul and an artist from the Blue Mountains, Philip, who is accompanied by his wife Gloria. There's Annette, who has travelled with me once before on a Himalayan trek and has decided that walking and eating in France will be far less strenuous. She has brought some friends along and they are a very lively bunch. There's also a small band of women from Sydney who have taken overseas tours together before and within days I have dubbed them 'the bad girls' because they are always up to no good. It's hard to hear yourself think in the bus because there is so much animated talking and laughter.

The itinerary falls into place like clockwork. The plan is to stay in small hotels in four main townships – Cahors, Puy L'Eveque, Villefranche-du-Perigord and Gourdon – and to use these hotels as a base for day trips. Most mornings we go by bus to some beauty spot and walk for an hour or so, or tour a village or ancient fortified town (a bastide), and most days we take a picnic lunch. Christiane, from Le Relais, has undertaken the task of preparing these lunches. She has equipped us with large eskies to carry chilled rosé and iced water and a variety of cold meats, pâtés and salads with cheese and always something interesting and different for dessert. We carry rugs and huge paper bags stuffed with fresh baguettes. Jan and I have already picked out the picnic spots but we are quite flexible. If we suddenly spy a better place with a good view we simply stop the bus and throw down the rugs. Our bus driver, Pierre, speaks no English but Jan translates all his little anecdotes about the local area, snippets of information known only to locals that enrich our understanding of the lifestyle in this part of France.

A good rapport develops, and within just a few days Pierre is telling us saucy French jokes during our shared picnic lunches, with Jan having the unenviable task of translating them into the Australian idiom. Among other things we do a guided tour of Cahors city, which is one of the most ancient towns in all of Europe; it is pre-Roman, with an awesome number of historic buildings still intact. We visit Bonaguil Castle, one of the most impressive fortress structures in France, and we go on a farm tour to see the way tobacco is grown and dried in the region and how the dreaded foie gras is produced. Some of the women stay in the bus during this part of the tour; they have no desire to witness acts of cruelty on helpless birds.

The concept of having picnics during the day and saving the large multi-course meals for the evenings is just common sense. Jan and I decided that if we all sat around for hours eating and drinking in the middle of the day, nobody would feel much like participating in the afternoon's activities. However, we have made two exceptions. One day we eat a sit-down lunch at a ferme auberge (farmhouse hostel), the one that Jock and I visited two years before. Little has changed. By law a ferme auberge must produce 80 per cent of what is served at the table themselves: this means baking their own bread, making their own wines and aperitifs, preserving their own confit, growing their own vegetables and fruit and, in some instances, even making their own cheeses. This auberge is authentic in every sense. We are given a brief tour of the farm by one of the owners, who has quite good English. They also run their business as a horse-riding holiday farm; they have a great collection of handsome steeds and a barn that has been converted to motel-like accommodation.

We are ushered into a long, narrow room dominated by a very long trestle table. It can seat at least twenty people and we take up the entire room because Jock and his daughter Harriet, visiting from Australia, have decided to join us for the day. The furnishings are very plain – lino on the floor and a few dusty decorations. Everyone has a sip of the fruity aperitif but some people find it too overpowering and hand theirs over to Jock or me. We're accustomed to home-made alcohol. They bring out the soup in huge steaming serving bowls and the feast begins. The meal is served by the grandmother and a neighbour who has come in to help for the day. There is course after course – pâté/terrine/confit of duck/sautéed potatoes/green vegetables/salad/cheese and excellent tart for dessert. The wine bottles are replaced regularly with more local brew and we all sample the eau de vie (water of life) that is served with black coffee at the end. As the meal proceeds we get noisier and more hilarious and I am a concerned that our hostess will think us an uncouth rabble. But they join in the spirit of the occasion and by the end of the meal the children of the family are sitting with us and everyone joins in for a toast at the end.

The other restaurant lunch is at Mme Murat's, an experience that I don't want them to miss. As she opens only at lunchtime, Jan books a large table for us – it runs almost the entire length of the main room. The plan is to visit the local market at Prayssac during the morning then drive to Pomarede to the restaurant. From there we will walk through the woods to the village of Goujenac then cross-country to my village of Frayssinet, where I will serve afternoon tea or a drink, depending on the time of day we get there.

The morning market is very much a farmers' market, with great barrows of local produce but also a fish stall from Bordeaux and stall-holders selling plant seedlings and flowers, oysters and live poultry, and cheeses of every description. It's colourful and lively and very French. At this time of year there are not many tourists, so it gives us an opportunity to soak up the atmosphere of a genuine rural French marché.

The bus trip to Pomarede takes only fifteen minutes and we are seated at our table with a glass in our hands by midday. Jeanne and Sylvie are pleased to have so many Australians and have prepared a hearty lunch for us. There are two or three other long tables filled with workmen: the local road-working teams are there, several tables of electricians and the usual quota of truck drivers pausing for their ritual repast. Jock and Harriet have joined us again, along with Carole, who worked at Mme Murat's for many years when her children were growing up.

The meal starts off in sedate fashion but quickly degenerates as Jock demonstrates the chabrol, a traditional peasant custom of tipping red wine into the dregs of the soup bowl and then, with elbows on the table, drinking the mixture directly from the bowl. Within moments our Australian contingent are slurping their soup and wine from their bowls and causing a lot of hilarity among the tables of workers. One of our women asks Carole if she will approach the road-workers and ask if they would mind posing for photographs at the end of the meal. They cheerfully agree. There are lots of smiles, waves and winks being exchanged between burly men in overalls with dark stubbly chins and our middle-aged but attractive Australian women who are quaffing the red wine like it's going out of style and tucking into each course with gusto. It's all a bit of a riot. The weather has become very hot, so there are lots of red cheeks and sweaty brows. By the time the dessert arrives everyone is groaning, but they battle on regardless. The road-workers get up to leave and are pounced on by half a dozen of the women, including the 'bad girls', who pose with them for a series of photographs. Stocky road-workers line up with women's arms draped over their shoulders or firmly squeezing them around the waist. They don't look at all unhappy at the female attention. Flossie, ever present, regards the proceedings with a disdainful beady eye.

After coffee I remind the group that we are a 'walking tour' and that we need to get started, as it will take at least two hours to get to Frayssinet. They look appalled.

'We don't want to walk,' they cry. 'It's too hot!' What they really mean is that they have had far too much red wine and the prospect of weaving their way through the woods is too much for them.

Jan manages to track down Pierre, who brings the bus over and we travel in comfort to my little house, where I pour more drinks (as if we really need them). The group spends the afternoon exploring the village, visiting the old church, walking down to the cemetery and then back to Le Relais, where they have a few more drinks to round off the afternoon. Most of them dip out on the dinner that was organised for that evening, and they are still quite subdued the following morning. Just as well it's only picnic lunches from now on.

Philip the artist has been keeping a visual diary of our travels, with finely sketched impressions of the villages and churches that we visit and small portraits of people involved in the tour. He captures the essence of Jock with a glass of red wine in one hand at the ferme auberge, then Jan sitting on a picnic rug and me with my straw hat and cheesy smile. Even Flossie gets her own portrait. He also does a sketch of my village house, which is much more romantic than a photograph. At the end of the trip, back in Australia, Philip has a little book made up for each of us, providing the most evocative memories of the time we spent together.

The last three days of the tour are spent in Paris, visiting Monet's garden once again and seeing the city sights. Before we depart on this last leg of the tour we have a farewell dinner with Jan and Philippe at a fairly refined restaurant in Gourdon, and once again it's a dress-up affair. The outfits are outrageous and because the restaurant is several blocks from the hotel the group is forced to walk through the main streets of the town looking like nothing on earth. I'm not sure that some of these French townships are quite ready for an Australian invasion. By the end of dinner we have caused a scandal, with me again making an appearance in high-heeled boots and fishnet stockings, and I belatedly remember that this was the same hotel and restaurant where the maître d' looked down his nose at the prospect of accommodating a busload of Australians. He was, I realise in retrospect, quite correct in his appraisal of Australian tourists.

It's interesting to see how different Giverny looks in the autumn, with its spilling borders of nasturtiums, trees just beginning to turn autumnal red and asters in full bloom. Some of the group would have liked to spend a whole day there, or even two, but it's the usual two hours in and out. On the last day as we pack our bags I'm really sad to see them go. We've had such fun as a group but, more than that, I have enjoyed sharing with them the little-known region of France that I fell in love with two years ago.

31

Back in Australia David is struggling with the cold weather and the loneliness of running the farm on his own. He phones me almost daily for a chat and I can tell he's feeling anxious and unhappy. I wish he could get one of his film projects off the ground so that he would have a working focus and not be so worried about me all the time. During my long stay in France he produced two feature films and was so frantically busy and preoccupied that the time we spent apart passed very quickly. He is finding being alone now rather depressing, especially when I relate anecdotes of the fun we are having on the tour. Our neighbours Robert and Sue ask him over for a meal at least once a week and he also stays in town from time to time to have dinner with Miriam, Rick and our grandsons. At the weekends Aaron and Ethan are often there, so it's not as though he is entirely abandoned.

One morning he phones in great excitement. The goose who has been sitting on eggs for weeks has hatched out eight small greenish goslings. He's as proud as punch and takes on a very protective role towards them. Not that he needs to. Geese are efficient parents and this is probably where they get their reputation for being aggressive. A group of five adults form a tight circle around the tiny birds and there's no risk of anything ever happening to them. David can't even get close to them. He refers to them as 'my babies' and when, one day, Ethan lets them out by mistake and they get under the fence and into Russell's old farm, David is distraught. Perhaps he just doesn't have the right temperament to be a goose farmer – he's too passionate and emotional – but they are eventually rounded up and from that moment he watches them day and night. I wonder if I will ever be allowed to do what I set out to – that is, render them down for goose fat. I doubt it.

After the tour I have about ten days to recover before setting off for Canada. There's a lot to do, because we have decided to go ahead with a downstairs renovation in our little house. An English designer, Tony, who has lived and worked in the Middle East for two decades, has recently moved to this region with his wife Terry, and has drawn up a set of plans for a new kitchen and living area. It is a simple but imaginative use of the limited space and we have decided to proceed although David and I are both rather worried about the cost. Unlike some people with second houses in France, we don't have vast amounts of cash to throw around and, with all the costs involved in getting the farm up and running in Australia, the house in France must take second place. Our friend Bob, who lives up the road, will do the floor replacement, but we are still uncertain about finding a builder to instal the kitchen. Having renovations done in a foreign country is a minefield in every sense; anyone who has undertaken such a task will attest to that. Even if you are there in person to supervise, things can go drastically wrong. So when you walk away and leave the whole project to trust in absentia the possibility of a disaster is greatly increased. We have heard so many horror stories of roofs that leaked, pipes that exploded and windows that were put in the wrong place. I shudder at the prospect but, because I have had detailed plans done, I feel confident that not *too* much can go awry. We know Bob very well and have shared many meals with him and his wife Carole, and they were both so kind to Ethan and Lynne during their stay in France that we are confident he will do a great job for us. Even before I leave, he tracks down some wide pine floorboards and we buy them immediately. It's difficult to get wide floorboards anywhere these days, and I am pleased that he has gone to the trouble of sourcing them for the project.

Jan and I take a trip by car to Toulouse with Margaret and their neighbour Sue to look at kitchens in, of all places, Ikea. It seems crazy on one level to buy a kit kitchen from Sweden when there are so many talented tradesmen in France and lots of interesting timbers to choose from, but there are far fewer carpenters around than there are projects to be built, so getting a good builder could mean waiting for months, or even years. I want this kitchen installed before David and I return next year, so I'd rather take the fast and easy option of choosing a kit. The Ikea store in Toulouse is about eight times the size of the one I have been to in Sydney and the range of kitchen styles and modules is mind-boggling. I have reached that stage of my life where I become impatient with too much choice – it overwhelms me and I become confused. So I select the style I like and throw the whole thing back at Tony the designer in the hope that he will pick the components that best suit the space.

Before I leave I am faced with the task of removing every object from the main room and carrying each one up two curved flights of stairs to the attic. There's the entire contents of the kitchen cupboards, the table and chairs, the cane furniture, the bookshelves, the rugs and all the bits and pieces that we have managed to accumulate in just over a year. In the midst of all this I am expecting a couple of Australian visitors, so I defer the operation, realising that if I don't, we won't be able to cook or sit in the living area or at the table to have meals. I am extremely fond of my friend but I don't know her new boyfriend very well and it's their first overseas trip, so I expect they will be tired and a little overwhelmed when they get to me.

This proves to be an understatement. They have just spent three weeks in the UK and then driven halfway across France to find me, getting lost along the way. They are exhausted and stressed and obviously, I quickly realise, having relationship problems. Now here I am, on the verge of an emotional time myself, going to meet my long-lost sister in Canada. I have survived a very rocky period in my marriage, finished an exhausting three-week stint leading the walking tour and am about to pack up my entire house and shift it up two flights of stairs. The very last thing I need is a couple of visitors intent on domestic rows right under my nose. But that's what happens.

There are tears and recriminations and their dispute spills out of the door onto the street and then around into the courtyard. It lasts for several hours and I am forced to keep a low profile by hiding in my bedroom. It's too ridiculous. I would have gone out and left them to it except that that very morning I had started the task of boiling up a huge vat of fig jam for Anthony, who has returned to England to sit some computer exams. He picked the figs from his two productive trees and started the initial stage of soaking the fruit in sugar overnight, but then ran out of time for the cooking stage. So I volunteered to cook and bottle the jam. It needs to be stirred every twenty minutes or so, which means I can't disappear. In the end my 'friends' resolve their differences but the jam has caught and turned black on the bottom of the pan. I bottle what I can save with slightly clenched teeth and look forward to them departing for the rest of their holiday and leaving me in peace.

I have heard many horror stories about 'guests from hell' from my friends in villages nearby. When you have a house in a faraway or highly sought after location, all sorts of friends and relatives descend, and the experience can either be pleasurable or frightful. Margaret Barwick told me about one old friend who came to stay and the two-week visit almost completely destroyed their previously harmonious relationship. This woman, who had worked with Margaret years before, married late and had her only child even later. As a mother she lacked common sense. The child, now aged four, entirely ruled the family, and it was impossible for Margaret and her friend to have even a brief conversation if the child was in the room. He would grab his mother's face and turn it away from Margaret, directing her attention back towards himself. He was obnoxious from the moment he opened his eyes in the morning until he eventually collapsed and fell asleep at night – usually very late because his parents hadn't yet developed a strategy for getting him off to bed. The worst aspect of the visit, however, was the child's odd toileting behaviour. He simply refused to sit on a potty or go anywhere near a toilet, and when he needed to defecate, the procedure was to spread a towel on a bed, where he would lie and perform his business with his legs in the air. All too bizarre for words.

Jock once had some visitors who brought along a single, middle-aged female friend who decided, after a few days, that Jock was marriageable material. He just needed a bit of tidying up and organising. This woman spent the entire three weeks of her visit clinging to Jock's side like a limpet, grinning gormlessly at him and winking lasciviously whenever she caught his eye. He felt extremely uncomfortable. Worse still, she decided to try to clean up his act. Every time he poured himself a glass of wine she would carp at him.

'Jock, Jock, darling you *drink* too much. It's not good for you. Don't have any more. You've had enough.'

Of course, it had the effect of making him drink twice as much as he normally would. Which is quite a lot. She also tried to tidy up his appearance (an impossibility) and kept dropping heavy-handed hints about staying indefinitely, perhaps for ever.

When she left, Jock collapsed in a state of relief. It was a lucky escape. I also recall a friend who visited regularly from America when we were living in Leura. This man, although charming in many respects, had the irritating habit of helping himself to the contents of our fridge, especially if he came home late at night and wanted a snack before retiring to bed. Many times I went to prepare a meal only to discover that half the ingredients had been devoured by our guest.

One morning at breakfast he complained bitterly to me that the stew he had half-eaten the night before, long after David and I had gone to bed, was tasteless and in fact had a very odd and unpleasant flavour. I shrieked with delight. In those days Muriel was still around, and she routinely cooked up a large vat of stew for the dog. It was a combination of kangaroo meat, brown rice and vegetables, usually the ones from the bottom of the vegetable bin, the ones that had gone a bit limp and bedraggled. It certainly contained no salt or anything to brighten up the flavour. The dog loved it just the way it was. I was delighted to inform my ill-mannered guest that he'd scoffed the dog's dinner. Sad to say, it didn't cure him of his irritating habit.

So there's a minefield of potential problems to be tackled when it comes to inviting friends to stay. Some guests are terrific. They arrive laden with goodies from the market and bottles of wine; they help with the cooking and do the washing up; they disappear for long periods to do their own thing without expecting to be 'entertained'; they strip the beds when they leave, even put the washing through the machine and hang it on the line before they depart. But these guests are few and far between. I resolve to be more careful, knowing that my times here in France, when I am here alone or with David, are precious and not to be wasted coping with other people's problems.

I am aware that David's anxiety is largely due to his concern that during this short period of time between finishing the tour and flying to Canada I will somehow re-establish my relationship with the man from Toulouse. Although I think about him a lot, I have absolutely no intention of making contact. We have agreed that silence between us is the best way of dealing with the finality of the relationship.

It doesn't work. Knowing that I am back in France and alone, he phones me. All the old feelings come flooding back. I find it difficult to breathe during our conversation and when he suggests I come to Toulouse for lunch I readily agree. Having been convinced in my heart that we had reached a mutual conclusion to the relationship I now feel we are back to square one.

I am torn about how to handle the situation. Part of me thinks that if David doesn't know it will be better for all concerned, but the other part of me knows I cannot lie to him now. Our marriage would be doomed.

So I tell David what I am doing and I go to Toulouse, just once. It's the final farewell, which I even jokingly refer to as the Last Tango in Toulouse. The reunion is bittersweet. We talk through all the good aspects of our brief relationship but also discuss the downside. I tell him in detail about David's reaction when I returned to Australia and about the pain it has caused my family. We agree that it simply isn't worth it and we agree that, once and for all, this should be the last time we see each other. This time I don't feel the same sensation of loss or grief. I have moved on and, although I feel a deep attachment to this man because what passed between us was so tender, I know that my heart is with David and our family.

I get back to the house in Frayssinet late in the evening and as I walk in the door the phone rings. It's David, and he sounds terrible. He's phoning from hospital in Bathurst where he has been admitted through the emergency department with an acute infection in his upper jaw. He had a tooth extracted several days before, and despite taking antibiotics his face has blown up and the infection has become serious. He was told by the admitting doctor that if he hadn't come in for urgent treatment the infection could have been fatal.

Despite his incredible physical pain he has only one question to ask: 'Is it over?'

'Yes, it's finished,' I reply.

'Are you sure?'

'I've never been more certain about anything in my life.'

When he starts to cry, I am overwhelmed, for the first time, with terrible feelings of guilt. While I realise that the infection is the direct result of a physical problem, I also acknowledge that he probably succumbed because of the intense stress he was experiencing, knowing that I was in Toulouse for the day, meeting my lover. I can do little but reassure him that the affair has finally been laid to rest and ask him to believe me. He has suffered enough.

It's still dark when Jan and Philippe arrive to drive me to Gourdon to catch the early train to Paris for my journey to Canada. The house echoes strangely because of the emptiness left after removing everything from the main ground level, and I feel almost bereft leaving it looking so bare and vulnerable. It will be totally transformed by the time I return.

The whole business of living in two countries is very difficult. While there is the joy of the diversity – the different friends I love in each place and the beauty that I relish in both France and Australia – there's an element of sadness each time I pack up and leave. I won't be seeing Jan or any of our gang again until the middle of next year, and yet I will soon be home again with David and the children and grandchildren. I feel torn. In between, I am going to meet my sister, and the thought of it overwhelms me.

I have spoken to Margaret only twice on the phone since we first started communicating last December. The first time was when Jon was visiting on his way to France. I thought it would be a good time to exchange our first words, knowing that Jon would be there beside her. It takes me all my courage to dial the number. In fact, I dial two or three times then hang up before it starts ringing. I am worried that I might cry, and that would be embarrassing for everyone. I sense from Margaret's letters that she isn't anticipating any sort of overly emotional reunion. She's certainly very pleased to be seeing Jon and me after all this time, but she quite obviously doesn't want the situation to escalate into high drama. Neither do I, although I feel deeply emotional about the prospect of meeting her and talking over all the memories and sensitive topics that are bound to arise. When I first hear Margaret's voice I am amazed. She sounds a lot like me and hasn't a trace of a Canadian accent – indeed, she still sounds fiercely Australian. I find it very reassuring. She also exudes warmth and humour over the telephone. She jokes with Jon and I speak with him briefly; he sounds tired, and I expect he must be feeling both physically and emotionally exhausted.

The next time I phone is a few days before I leave Frayssinet, to make sure we have communicated clearly and that she and Ken will be picking me up from the airport at Victoria. I am concerned about the lateness of the flight but she reassures me that it's no trouble at all. They are both very excited about seeing me.

From Paris I fly to Montreal, where I change flights for Vancouver. From there to Victoria is just a twenty-minute flight. The airport at Vancouver is virtually deserted when my plane lands, and it takes me a few minutes to find my way to the transfer desk and work out where the small plane is leaving from. My luggage has been booked right through, but I have only a few minutes to get myself from one side of the terminal to the other. The booking clerk looks at my ticket, then at me. 'Can you run, lady?' he asks.

'If I have to.'

'Well, off you go. Gateway 22. They'll be waiting for you, I hope,' he smiles.

So I run like a madwoman down the long corridors of this half-deserted airport. Running to meet Margaret. I don't know whether to laugh or cry – after fifty years of wanting to meet her I'm running like fury to catch the plane. It's the dash of my life.

I make it and the flight feels as if it is over almost before it began. We barely reach our cruising altitude before we have to descend. I pick up my bag and walk out through the arrival gates. I catch a glimpse of Margaret from inside the arrival area, picking her out instantly from the photographs she sent me. I feel a shock of recognition. She is intently searching the face of each passenger who arrives. There is something so familiar about her facial expression but I know it can't be my memory of her because I was less than eighteen months old when she fled our family home. She looks at me but doesn't react until I call out her name. She then smiles and we embrace just for a moment. I then see Ken, who is very tall and has a grin on his face. I give him a big hug, too, and we go straight out to the car to head back to their farm. In the back seat is Sidney, their geriatric Newfoundland dog, who puffs and pants and fills the car with his warm doggy breath.

We are all very tired and, after a cup of tea and a bit of a chat, we head off to bed. I sleep well and wake the next morning to the smell of pancakes cooking. It's Sunday and pancakes are a tradition. Over breakfast they fill me in on the plans for the next few days. Monday is Thanksgiving Day in Canada, and some of

Ken's family will be coming for dinner – they will cook a large turkey for the traditional celebration. On Wednesday Margaret's painting group will be coming to the house. This is a group of about twenty women artists who meet once a week at each other's homes to paint and have lunch together. They have been meeting for years, and some of them have travelled with Margaret and Ken to France, to the Lot. They have driven through my village, I feel certain. And they know the region and love it well.

In between times Margaret plans to take me on a few tours around the area, to the Buchardt Gardens and on a scenic drive around Victoria, which is a historically significant city. I have only four days and we should make the most of them.

I realise, from the moment I first meet them, that Margaret and Ken are a very united and private couple. Even though they have busy and full lives, there is a calm, unhurried air about the way they do things. I am impatient to get Margaret talking, to draw out as much information as I can about what she remembers of her childhood and how she felt about leaving the family behind, but I sense that she can't be pushed in any way. I may be her sister but she doesn't know me and I have no right to expect her to open up immediately or to talk about memories that she might find painful or confronting. So I just go with the flow and enjoy their company, trying to get to know them a little without applying any pressure or having unrealistic expectations.

We take a leisurely walk around the house and then the farm. The house nestles behind a lofty hedge of conifers which have grown from small seedlings, they tell me, in the twenty years since they built the house. Although Canadian in design, with a deep storage cellar and central heating and well-insulated walls and windows, it has the ambience of an Australian farmhouse because of the way it sits close to the ground and because it also has deep, shady verandahs. Inside, it is decorated not unlike my own home and this intrigues me – the same sort of old-fashioned but comfortable furniture, a house designed for living in rather than for show. The main difference is the artwork. Where my house is decorated with movie posters from David's numerous films over the years, Margaret and Ken's walls are covered with artwork, many of the paintings done by Margaret herself over the years. I recognise the style from the one painting she left behind as a teenager. It's now in the home of my brother Dan.

There are lots of photographs of Ken's family. His parents and grandparents and aunts and cousins are well represented, and there are also shots of Ken and Margaret on their various overseas holidays, mostly in France. There is not one single photograph of Margaret's family, but I know why. She didn't take any family photographs when she left, just a small suitcase with a few clothes and her painting materials. That was all of her first life that she could carry on foot as she escaped the madness that was her family home, and mine.

The farm is small but efficiently organised. Ken has a richly productive vegetable garden and he enters his crops every year at the local agricultural show. He's a prominent local farmer, involved in several agricultural committees in the region. It's the end of the season and most of the vegetable crops have been harvested, but the main crop, kiwi fruit, is still ripening on the vine. I have never seen full-scale kiwi fruit production and I am impressed at how attractive they are en masse. A huge area has symmetrical trellises smothered in a brilliant green canopy, with thousands of almost-ripe furry Chinese gooseberries waiting to be picked. They grow two varieties: most are 'Hayward', the same variety that is commercially popular in Australia, the others are 'Ananaja', commonly called grape kiwi fruits. They are the size of a grape, with a smooth skin, and are eaten whole, skin and all. They are delicious. I've never seen them before and feel certain they're not available in Australia. I am determined to find out when I return.

In between trips out and about exploring the island Margaret and I spend precious time sitting in the family room, drinking tea and talking. It's good to talk. The look of familiarity that I detected when I first saw her at the airport still plagues me, and it takes me days to work out what it is. She looks a lot like our father, around the mouth and jaw in particular. She also has the most startling light-green eyes. I can't take my eyes off them and I ask her about them.

'From my mother, apparently,' she responds. She has no idea what her mother looked like and can't remember seeing any photographs.

We gradually open up and talk about our respective childhoods. Her quiet, calm reminiscences make so much come alive for me and help explain many things that have been a mystery to me.

Margaret believes she was only about four years old when her mother committed suicide. She can't quite remember and she certainly can't remember at what age she first became aware of her mother's cause of death. It may not have been, she thinks, until she was an adult. She recalls being looked after by various relatives in the following years, including for a while our father's sister Melissa. Our father Theo married Muriel Angel, my mother, when she was twenty-one and Margaret was eight or nine years old. That part of it is all a bit of a blur.

During the war years they all lived in America – Theo, Muriel, Jon and Margaret. There were endless fights and brawls, the result of heavy drinking by both parents. Muriel frequently sported a black eye or a bruised arm and Margaret recalls that she often tried to break up these violent fights but never succeeded. It was a lost cause.

Back in Australia, after the war, my mother gave birth to two children in fairly rapid succession – first Dan and then me. Our flat was small. It had only two bedrooms, one for Mum and Dad and one for Jon, so Margaret had no choice but to share a small glassed-in sunroom with Dan, who was a toddler, and then me as well, from the time I was born. She had no wardrobe or chest of drawers of her own – clothes were kept at one end of Jon's wardrobe. She described how difficult it was, as a teenage girl, dressing and undressing every day with no privacy.

I remember from my own childhood how our flat was always untidy and often dirty because Muriel loathed housework apart from cooking and ironing. Margaret confirmed this and added more to the picture. It appears that our father had several love affairs when Muriel was pregnant and nursing young babies. Her way of dealing with the situation was to drink, and to drink quite heavily. Margaret recalls that for much of the time when Dan and I were very young our mother was sipping sherry all afternoon, then fighting with our father when he got home from work. Margaret was in high school and at one point Theo had a brilliant idea. She should leave school and stay at home with Muriel, helping to run the house and look after us small children. Margaret was devastated. The years in America had set

LAST TANGO IN TOULOUSE

both Margaret and Jon back academically because of the very different standards of education – Australia's standard was quite a bit higher. She had just started to catch up and excel at school, and now she was told she had to leave and stay home to wipe babies' bottoms and clean up the continuous mess that was our chaotic environment.

She went to school and informed her headmistress that she would have to leave at the end of the term. Outraged, this feisty woman asked for our father's phone number at work and promptly called him. There was never again a mention of Margaret leaving school. When she related this story it didn't really surprise me. Our father, for all his violent temper and bullying attitude, was a weak man, spineless. I can imagine the headmistress ringing him in indignation, defending Margaret's right to a decent education, and him backing down immediately. It made me even more furious with him than I was on my own and my mother's behalf.

It also highlighted for me the hypocrisy of my father's so-called political ideals. He often spoke of the importance of equal rights for women. We were told about the wonderful work of the suffragettes and how women must continue to fight for equal pay and recognition. But in truth our father had the most appalling attitude to women. The way in which he treated both his wives, with violence and a total disregard for their needs and their feelings, was deplorable. I recall as a child having no pressure placed on me to achieve academically whereas my brother Dan was constantly being urged to top the class. Margaret says the situation was the same for her.

Margaret also tells some humorous anecdotes at which we share a good laugh – even though, in many ways, the events weren't very funny. It seems that our father's spending on his own clothes, on alcohol and tobacco, on gambling and other women left very little over for domestic purposes or the comforts of life. Muriel never had shoes, Margaret recalled. For years she wore the same pair of sandals, winter and summer. There was only one towel in the bathroom for the whole family to use and if you were the last in line for a shower – which Margaret often was – it was wringing wet. Every week the housekeeping money would run out by Wednesday and our father didn't get paid until Friday night. So Muriel would lug the family set of silver cutlery and two silver vases up the steep hill to Spit Junction to a pawn shop. There she would get enough money to buy food and booze and cigarettes for the rest of the week. On Saturday morning she would reclaim the silverware and they would once again have knives and forks to eat with.

When Margaret got her first holiday job, the very first thing she did was go to Nock and Kirby's to buy a set of basic cutlery so that on Wednesdays, Thursdays and Fridays the family didn't have to eat dinner with their fingers.

Margaret left home because conditions in our family were untenable for an intelligent and creative young woman. She waited until her eighteenth birthday because, legally, that was the youngest age at which a child could leave home then. She didn't want a fuss and she certainly didn't want the indignity of being dragged back home by the police. She spent the last few years, from sixteen to eighteen, quietly telling herself that it wouldn't be long now, that she would be free very soon. She was a calm, level-headed young woman and had obviously already developed such inner strengths and qualities of character that she was going to survive no matter what.

As we talk I try my best not to show the emotions I feel as each new story emerges. I want to keep our time together as happy and stress-free as possible. When I feel myself losing it a little, I go to my room for 'a rest' so that I can have a quiet cry to myself without upsetting anybody. I feel overjoyed that I am here at last with my sister, but also deeply sad that we have, through no fault of our own, missed out on a whole lifetime together. I don't know whether I am feeling anger or pain. Both, I guess. I am overwhelmed by the knowledge that, for me, being here is the realisation of a lifelong dream. David and our children all know. I have so often said to them, 'One day I am going to find Margaret.' And now I have.

What intrigues Margaret is my knowledge of her as a child and teenager. She is quite honest with me from the start, saying that she barely remembered me. I was only fourteen months old when she left and by that time she was at teacher's college and working, spending as little time as possible in the cramped flat. I was just a blur in her memory. But my impressions of my older sister have been firmly set for as long as I can remember. It would have been my mother who gave me such a strong image of Margaret. Muriel excelled as family storyteller. She regaled me with stories of the years the family had spent in America before Dan and I were born. She peppered these stories with imagery and detail, describing the clothes they wore and the food they ate and the picture-postcard snowy white Christmases they had when living in Connecticut. I knew the names of all the cats they'd had and of their neighbours and friends, and in many ways I felt as though I'd been there myself, so vivid were my mother's word pictures. There were also photographs, of course. Black and white images of Jon and Margaret from the ages of about nine and ten, standing together on street corners in New York and outside their white clapboard house in New Canaan. It wasn't until I was much older that Mum told me about the dark side of their life – the fights and the drinking and the violence, in painful detail. So for me, Margaret has always been there, even though for her I was just a shadow from the life she was trying to forget. I know that I used to fantasise as a child, when things were really difficult at home, that perhaps Margaret might come back one day and rescue me, take me away to wherever she had escaped to. And that I, too, would be free. But those were just childish dreams. However, I never gave up hope that some day I would find Margaret and, now, here I am in her house with her husband and floppy dog. It's a very significant few days in my life.

As the days go by I realise how much alike we are in so many ways. We talk alike and we both have a well-developed, rather outrageous sense of humour. We look alike at certain moments and Ken quite proudly shows me a photograph taken of Margaret when she was just a few years younger than I am now. The resemblance is undeniable. But it's more than that. We like doing the same sorts of things. Margaret likes to make jellies and jams and preserves from all the fruits, wild and cultivated, around the farm and the surrounding countryside. She has a special cooker for extracting the essential juices from soft fruit that I am greatly taken with. We go together in search of one at the hardware store; I buy one and will carry it home as hand luggage. I have been making jellies and preserves for years and this cooker will make the task much easier. Margaret loves gardens and trees and makes the most wonderfully worm-rich compost for Ken's prize-winning vegetable garden. Making compost has always been one of my great passions too. My kids once dubbed me 'Queen of the Compost' and the title stuck. I take a photograph of my big sister adding scraps to her compost heap. It makes me laugh to think of it. Margaret and Ken are both passionate conservationists. They belong to an organisation that is fighting overdevelopment of their quiet rural area. She distributes badges and leaflets and attends meetings to try to stop the threat of carving up the farmland into small housing estates. I tell her about the battles I have fought over the years to prevent overdevelopment in the Blue Mountains, the fights against subdivisions and corrupt local councillors and against McDonald's (most of these battles now lost, I'm sad to say). She applauds my activism and I applaud hers.

We get out the map of France and they show me all the villages where they have stayed over the years. By following the road systems I realise that they would, indeed, have driven right past my front door on at least two occasions, but that would have been long before we bought the house. Margaret loves animals, and of course, so do I. The parallels go on and on. Then something dawns on me and I laugh out loud.

'You know, Margaret, it isn't really surprising that we are so much alike. Just think about it. We share the genes of the same father. That is an inescapable fact. But when you think about it, we also had virtually the same childhood. Just a whole generation apart. Your childhood was more tragic because your mother died; at least I always had my own mother. And of course she was the woman who raised you from the age of eight until eighteen. We really had almost exactly the same early life experiences; the only difference was we didn't have them together.'

It's true. We are linked by a common thread that is tragic but also beautiful. I am so grateful that I have been able to find her.

It seems appropriate that I am here with Margaret and Ken on Thanksgiving Day. Even though it isn't a tradition celebrated in Australia, I know enough about it to realise that for us, as sisters, today has special significance. We start early to prepare the evening feast. There's quite a bit of cooking to do and there will be eight guests for dinner. I discuss with Margaret my technique for cooking turkey. This involves filling it with the traditional stuffing but putting it in the oven upside down, with the breast underneath, until the last half hour when it is turned over so the skin on the breast can turn brown and crispy. She laughs and says it must be because I'm Australian and they do everything upside down in Australia. She charges me with responsibility for the turkey and we work together all afternoon, preparing vegetables, organising dessert, setting the table and doing all the thousand and one little chores associated with a large family celebration.

The magic of this day, for me, is how well we work together in the kitchen; just like sisters, in fact. We don't trip over each other or get under each other's feet. Margaret has no problem dele-gating tasks to me and giving me the run of her domain. As we cook we talk more about our mad family and our sad childhoods, but we also laugh a lot and make jokes and enjoy the spirit of the occasion. I wish that we could have done this many times before, but it wasn't meant to be. This is our time now and we must make the most of it.

Ken's family arrive and it becomes a high-spirited and happy evening. They are all intrigued to meet me. They have known and loved Margaret for thirty-five years and to all intents and purposes she has never had another family. Some have asked about her background over the years but she always swept the questions aside with good humour. She must have had a family at some stage, but not one that she chose to talk about. Ken knew, of course, but it was a story they shared and kept very much to themselves. As we sit down to eat – the turkey a triumph – Ken's cousin says a brief prayer of thanks, then Ken stands up and makes a little speech of thanksgiving for 'the sisters long apart and now reunited'. We raise our glasses and say the toast. 'To the sisters now reunited.' Somehow I manage not to cry.

33

 My few days in Canada are intense – more sightseeing, more talking, more laughter. We start to feel more relaxed and open in each other's company and the breaks we take to explore Vancouver Island help to balance the intensity of our conversations. Each morning Ken and I set off early and take old Sidney for a walk around the block. He's very, very slow, shuffling along and puffing furiously, but it affords important time for Ken and me to talk about the sadness of the early life Margaret and I both share, and to get to know each other a little better. He has a slow, warm way of talking and his view of life is very soothing to me. The days flash past quickly. Margaret takes me to see Victoria University, where she once taught, and the flat, overlooking the water, where she and Ken lived, when they were first married. We have lunch together in a restaurant on a jetty and also in a pub that serves good local beer.

On my last day we get ready for the arrival of the painting group. It's just a matter of clearing all the surface areas, tables and benches and card tables to create working areas for each person's project. We set up cups and saucers for tea and coffee; masses of food will be brought, as it's very much a communal gathering. They are an interesting group of women. Widely varied in age and background and from many different countries, they share a common passion for art and good company. They have all been told that Margaret's sister will be in residence and most are amazed because, once again, they were not aware that Margaret had any siblings or indeed any family at all. They greet me as though I really am a long-lost sister, their sister as well as Margaret's. There are hugs and a few tears and they all want to know everything about me – who I am, where I have sprung from, all about my life and family. Margaret seems very proud of me, which thrills me to bits. She tells them of my adventures in France and of my trekking, reminding me that I am about to leap from this emotional reunion to Kathmandu. No wonder I feel a little overwhelmed. We have cups of tea, then lunch is spread out on the table. Homemade breads and salads and local smoked salmon – it's a feast, and for me it's a joy to be included.

Mid-afternoon, it's time for me to go. Ken has decided to let Margaret take me to the airport alone so that we can share those last few minutes together. We get there ahead of time and the check-in desk says I can catch an earlier flight, which means we don't have time to stand around and chat. Just enough time to hug and say goodbye.

We agree that it has been an amazing time for both of us. We keep emotions very low-key, but as I turn to leave, Margaret says so sweetly, 'I'm really sorry to see you go.'

I save my tears for the plane.

On the long flight home I am armed with my sleeping pills and a good book to read. It's all a bit strange, because I will have just one night in Sydney at a hotel before picking up my small trekking group to go to Kathmandu and from there on up into the Himalayas. David is coming down from the farm to spend this one night with me and we will swap luggage. I have already packed my trekking needs – backpack, thermal underwear, medicines, torch and walking boots. I will give him my more glamorous French country clothes in return for my practical adventuring gear.

I am feeling emotionally exhausted but also deeply happy and satisfied with this extraordinary family connection. I am sitting beside a Canadian woman, perhaps a couple of years older than I am, and we exchange polite greetings as we settle into our seats. I find that tears keep welling up in my eyes as we take off, and when I look round, she is crying too. After take-off a member of the cabin crew comes and touches her arm and speaks softly to her. I hear the word 'Bali' and I wonder if there is a connection. While I have been with Margaret in Canada the Bali bombings have taken place, and it has been frustrating trying to get much news of it on Canadian television. It didn't assume the same level of prominence as in Australia.

Seeing the tears trickling down the cheeks of the woman beside me, I decide to ask.

'Do you have someone injured in Bali?'

'My son, Rick,' she says. 'He has burns to 45 per cent of his body. He's in a Melbourne hospital and I am on my way to see him.'

Over the next twelve hours Audrey and I talk and cry together and sometimes, through sheer exhaustion, sleep. She tells me all about Rick. He's thirty-two and a much loved son. An adventurer and traveller, always. He has spent his young adult life working in good jobs for two or three years at a time and saving his money. He then takes off for two or three years, and has covered an enormous number of countries in his travels. He writes frequent letters home and phones regularly. Audrey reads me his last letter, written from Bali, and shows me photographs of his smiling open face.

She is curious about my trip to Canada and I tell her all about our mad, sad family and about finding my sister Margaret after fifty years. My story makes her cry too.

It's been a struggle for Audrey to get on this plane at such short notice. She didn't have a current passport and finding the money for the airfare was very difficult. Friends and family came to the rescue, and both the Australian and Canadian governments have also swung into action with assistance. She will be met by officials at Sydney airport and taken quickly to a plane headed for Melbourne. Her son didn't get much medical assistance during the critical first twelve hours after the explosion. Now, however, he is in the best of care, but his condition is critical. He is being kept artificially in a coma to help his body deal with the shock and pain. Audrey is hoping, desperately, that when he is gradually brought out of the coma he won't have suffered brain damage too. But it's on the cards.

34

 In our Sydney hotel room I sleep the sleep of a soul totally drained of all energy and emotion. David is concerned about me because I seem so flat, but by the next day I am feeling more bouncy and start to repack for the evening flight to Nepal. We have a delightfully happy day together: we go out for lunch and walk along the foreshore of Botany Bay and spend the entire afternoon in bed. David has recovered from his dramatic jaw infection but is understandably doubtful about my change of heart in seeing the man from Toulouse one last time. He will need plenty of reassurance and love from me to regain his confidence. I don't think I fully appreciated just how shattering this whole experience has been for him; I realise it is going to take a long time for him to trust me again. He may never do so.

I am amazed that I'm not feeling sad any more: not about the man from Toulouse nor about my sister. I just feel a great sense of relief. It's as though I have been walking on a long tightrope and I'm now, finally, back on firm ground. Although I am here in Australia with David for just this brief moment, I know that in two weeks I will be back home for six whole months at the farm and that life will somehow get back to normal.

As we doze together on the bed in the afternoon before leaving for the airport, I think about the thirty-one years we have been together. It hasn't all been bad – in fact, a lot of it has been terrific. David is a good man. He loves me and together we love what we have created: a large and happy family. For perhaps the first time I can acknowledge properly his role in making it all work – a very different role from mine, but no less valid. We have survived this long together, and we will stick with it until the end.

For the third time this year I am to meet up with a tour group. This time it's a small band of trekkers and two of them, Helen and Rose, have been on a Himalayan tour with me before, so it's a bit like a family reunion. This will be my first time in Nepal; my other treks were in the alpine valleys of northern India, so I am looking forward to seeing a different region of this flora-rich mountain range. There are six women and one man on the trip and we meet in Kathmandu two days before heading off to Pokhara and then, on foot, up towards the Annapurnas and Machapuchare, a sacred mountain also known as Fishtail because of its unusual pointed shape.

One of the group, Cheryl, is an Englishwoman who has booked through the travel company's London office. This is a first for me, because all my previous groups have been from Australia. As usual, I have moments of concern, in the first day or so, about the ability of the group to become cohesive, but these fears are quickly dispelled as we start to climb and get to know each other a little better. Another of our band, Ros, is seventy-one years old. This is not all that rare. I have trekked to quite high altitudes with keen bushwalkers in their mid-seventies. However, it's difficult to tell just how well each person understands how challenging the trek will be at times. Helen and Rose are well aware that walking uphill for seven hours a day, at altitude, is pretty hard work – and several of the others have also done difficult walks before. People who book on these trips are usually highly motivated individuals who like to push themselves a little and aren't afraid of stepping outside their comfort zone. Aching limbs, blistered feet and freezing overnight temperatures are all part of the experience and usually it's mental fortitude rather than fitness level that gets people through.

Our local trip leader, Rupan, is enthusiastic and everyone takes to him immediately. The sherpas and porters and cooks are also very friendly and seem to be enjoying themselves in spite of the huge packs they carry all day and the work that's required of them when camp is set up every afternoon. We carry just daypacks, with a bottle of water, a camera, loo paper and the odd packet of boiled sweets. All the rest of our gear is carried for us, and by the time we reach camp, usually mid-afternoon, the tents are up, the kettle is on and afternoon tea is about to be served. For an 'adventure' holiday it's about as comfortable as it gets.

It's a good thing for complacent middle-class Westerners, such as us, to visit countries like India and Nepal, to remind ourselves of how most of the rest of the world lives – basically, in poverty and hardship. Nepal is one of the poorest countries in the world, and for many of the people we encounter on the trek, living in small villages dotted along our walking route, life is pretty tough. As we walk up the mountain tracks together we talk a lot about all these issues, about local politics, ethics, the environment, medical and health issues and general humanity. It's an integral part of trekking in a third world country. Instead of sitting in an air-conditioned bus and seeing the broad sweep of a foreign country, you are down at ground level, walking through villages and beside fields of wheat and potatoes and stopping and meeting and talking with people and really getting a feel for the place. This is enriched by the relationships that naturally develop between members of the tour and also with the local crews. It's a sort of bonding: we are undertaking something that is essentially challenging, and we are sharing the experience. For example, the sherpa guides immediately recognise that Ros is older than the others and two of them stick to her like glue, offering moral and physical support as we climb. She's a cheerful person and never complains once about the difficulties or the tough terrain.

Rose has just spent a month visiting family and friends in England. When one friend heard that she was heading off to the Himalayas on a trek, she commented in awe, 'How thrilling! And tell me, are the Himalayas steep?'

'Only about 28,000 feet steep,' was Rose's reply. And it becomes the catchcry of our little team. Every time we arrive, puffing and panting, at a small clearing we look at each other and say, 'Are the Himalayas steep?

Helen and Graham are a married couple having their first long overseas trip together without their teenage children, so it's quite special for them too. There's a period of about ten days when we are totally out of range of any form of communication – no email or phones high in these mountains, and it's hard to be completely out of contact with your family. Especially if it's the first time. The last member of the group, Diane, has a fairly high-pressure job back in Australia and the trek is for her a real escape from normal life. Unfortunately she develops a serious cold on the second day that will make the climb more difficult for her than for the rest of us. The air thins as we climb and we all need as much oxygen in our lungs as we can get, so having her nasal passages blocked and inflamed makes it really tough going.

On our third day of walking, Rupan asks if we object to making the day a little longer by setting up camp in an alternative site which is about an hour further along the track from the original site designated in our trip notes. We have a little meeting and, although I am concerned about Diane having to walk the extra distance when she is so unwell, we agree to the change. I am also a bit worried about Helen, who injured her back in Kathmandu before we set out. She saw a physiotherapist in Pokhara who recommended that she really shouldn't do the walk at all, but she's a feisty woman and doesn't want to miss out. One of the sherpas is carrying her day-pack to make her progress less painful. After lunch we continue walking and, as the hours pass, I wonder when we will reach the camp. We have passed through the original 'forest camp' and, instead of continuing up the side of the mountain, we seem to be descending. By four o'clock alarm bells are ringing in my head and I detect a certain tension between the lead sherpa and those in the middle of the group. They are shouting back and forth to each other in Nepalese and I have a strong sense that there is a heated disagreement about the direction we have taken. Our leader suddenly calls for us all to stop. There's a lot of talking and dashing back and forth along the track, which is very poorly defined. Eventually, we have to acknowledge among ourselves that we are well and truly lost.

At this stage we are sitting in a tiny clearing, and as the light fades the temperature drops dramatically. All we are wearing are our day clothes, which are fairly lightweight because walking, even through the vast rhododendron forests, can be hot work in the middle of the day. We all have water bottles although these have been pretty much drained because of the extra hours of walking, and we have all carried a warm jacket or waterproof coat in case of rain. Other than that, we have nothing. No food (apart from half a packet of sultanas and nuts which I found in my pack and some English sweets carried by Cheryl), no spare water, no torches, no thermal underwear, no sleeping bags, no tents. Most of us don't even have torches, but Helen, our most experienced trekker, has carried waterproof matches and a whistle. We light a fire and huddle around it, every so often blowing our whistle and calling out 'COOOOOEEEE' pathetically into the darkness. Our sherpas are still scurrying hither and thither trying to find the right trail, but without success. We have obviously walked so far from the correct route that they won't be able to find it in the dark. I have a short meeting with Rupan and we decide that we can't stay here all night. The clearing is too small and we are becoming damp as the overnight mist sets in. There is a rough shepherd's hut, just a thatched roof on four poles, further back up the track and we decide that we should walk back to it so that at least Ros, Diana and Helen can be made as comfortable as possible.

What follows is a nightmare. There are only four or five torches between thirteen people and the strongest beam must be given to the sherpa who is leading us back up the rough, ill-defined track. We hold hands and walk in a chain, very slowly, often slipping and falling and struggling in the dark. I cannot see my feet at all, and the only way I know where to place each foot as I climb is by watching the white sandshoes of the sherpa in front of me. I am the second in the chain. I am clinging to his hand for dear life, then clutching Rose, who has a wonderfully wacky sense of humour. We try, somehow, to keep this journey as light as possible, singing songs such as 'You'll Never Walk Alone', and cracking jokes and generally keeping our spirits up. But it's an arduous climb and I sense, further back down the line, quite a bit of fear. We could be walking like this all night if we take the wrong path again, and there's the added element of the sheer drop on one side that we remember from having walked down the mountain during the afternoon. Helen and Graham, in the middle, support Ros and Diane and Helen, who are finding the going very tough indeed. Diane in particular is struggling for breath. She can't even wipe her nose because we have all linked hands, so she is having to endure the situation with her nose and eyes streaming. The sherpas and Rupan are doing all they can to support us – they obviously feel very bad about getting us into this situation.

It takes a full two hours for us to reach the shepherd's hut in the dark, and there are tears of relief when we stagger into it. Exhausted, slightly dehydrated and freezing cold, we immediately light a fire and find whatever we can that's warm. There are two sleeping bags – some of the sherpas carry their own with them in their day-packs – and a silver space blanket in the emergency first aid kit. We wrap up as many people as possible and then wonder what we are going to do with ourselves until daybreak. It's 10 pm and the sun will not rise until just before 6 am. It's too cold to sit on the ground – within minutes the extremely low soil temperature seeps through our lightweight pants – so we have no alternative but to stand up. All night. Rose suggests we light a second fire, just outside the hut, and the sherpas do so. Legally, we are not allowed to use any of the timber in the forests for fires. There is so little left and what remains is essential for the local village people, but this is an emergency. Without the two fires we would be suffering even more discomfort, and I am seriously concerned that Diane may develop a secondary respiratory infection if she suffers from exposure.

It is the longest night of my life. I have stayed up all night before – for New Year's Eve parties in my youth – but that involved eating and drinking and dancing and snogging and sitting down a lot. This night is spent trying to remain upright and warm with dense wet smoke blowing into our eyes. Five of us remain this way all through the night, occasionally sitting down to rest momentarily. The Nepalese, tougher and more accus- tomed to the climate, manage to sleep fitfully on the cold hard ground by the fire. I don't know how they can do it. I can barely remain seated for five minutes without needing to jump up again and get warm. Helen, exhausted and with her back causing a lot of pain, also manages to sleep a little while Ros and Diane, warmly wrapped under the shelter, seem completely out to it. Very few jokes are being cracked and there are no cheery singsongs. It's just a matter of getting through it.

At sunrise we revive a little, build up the fires again and talk about how good that first cup of tea is going to taste. We talk about long hot baths and massages and toast and Vegemite. Our sherpas go out again looking for the track and they return, very quickly, with scouts from the main camp, who have been desperately worried and searching for us half the night. They walked all the way back to the last village in the dark and were very alarmed when the villagers said that three Maoist terrorists had been seen in the forest several days beforehand. Convinced we had been kidnapped, they fell upon us with cries of relief. Sadly, they are carrying no water or tea, but they do know the way to camp and so we pack up as best we can, trying not to leave too much mess for the shepherds, who will no doubt wonder who has been lighting fires inside their hut. Exhausted and, to some extent, suffering from exposure, we shuffle back up the track, relieved to be heading at last in the right direction. It's about two hours of walking but within forty minutes three of the cooking team suddenly appear with pots of steaming hot porridge, milk, tea and sugar and water. I realise that I can't face eating or drinking anything except water. I feel quite nauseous and, even though it would be a good to eat something, I believe I would throw up if I did. So I sip water and hope for the best.

We are greeted like heroes when we get to camp. Some of us just collapse into the tents without eating or drinking anything more. The kitchen crew want to make us breakfast – omelettes and toast – but by now we are all feeling a bit queasy. So they make aromatic clear soup with garlic and ginger. We sit in a daze sipping this comforting brew, then all go to our tents and sleep for most of the day. We are totally exhausted.

Late in the afternoon, as we rise, some locals arrive with cold beer to sell and we each buy a bottle. We sit around and discuss our 'adventure', a sort of debriefing. From some of the conversations that were held during the night and earlier this morning, I wouldn't be at all surprised if the group decides that we should now give up, turn back and return to Pokhara. I am particularly concerned that the overnight experience has been traumatic for

Ros and Diane, so their attitude will be critical to the group decision.

As we talk through the whole episode, step by step from when we first realised we were lost, a common theme emerges. Everyone is proud of the way we reacted to the situation. There was no anger and no blame and no panic. We came together as a group and supported each other through the experience. We agree that it has been an inspirational moment in our lives, a confirmation of the human spirit. Instead of wanting to turn round and go back, the group is even more enthusiastic about going onwards and upwards. I am pleased. Even though we have lost a day, which means we will spend only one night at the top camp, there is a strong will to continue.

The trekking doesn't get any easier and we are all still drained from our night sleeping (or rather standing) rough in the forest. But we spend the next two days continuing the walk until we get to a camp, perched above the cloudline on hard ground with very little vegetation. We have reached an altitude close to 4000 metres and the air feels very thin. Ros, in particular, finds breathing uncomfortable, and everyone has a slight headache. It's also very cold and misty although every so often it clears and we have uninterrupted views of Annapurnas and Machapuchare. The view of the surrounding mountains is so spectacular that, despite the difficulties, we now know exactly why we have come. You cannot find yourself in such a wild, remote and beautiful place without actually going through the pain and pleasure of walking there. We realise, as we stand in a huddle, sipping our hot tea, that very few people in the world ever make it to such a place. It's a rare privilege and none of us is taking the experience for granted. The sherpas are particularly proud of Ros, commenting that no seventy-one-year-old Nepali woman would climb to this altitude if she didn't need to, just to look at the view, as we are doing.

There is an optional extra climb the following morning, and we plan to start the downward trek after lunch. However, Ros and Diana are really feeling the effects of the altitude, so we split into three groups. They start the descent immediately after breakfast, the two Helens, Graham and Rose have a restful morning in camp and Cheryl and I do the optional extra climb. It's up a steep, sharp ridge to a plateau from where the views are even more spectacular. As we set out with our three sherpa companions, we meet a party of young trekkers coming down. One of them complains that the walk is absolutely terrifying and Cheryl and I exchange a nervous glance. But we are determined to proceed regardless.

The climbing is slow because Cheryl and I are experiencing slight breathing difficulties. The track falls away very steeply in several places and we have to keep our wits about us – and our balance. At one point we have to walk around a narrow rock shelf, clinging to a boulder as we go. I glance down briefly and realise just how far it would be to fall. I suddenly think of David and my children and grandchildren. They would be horrified if they could see where I am right now, clinging to a rock perilously perched on the edge of a sheer cliff. But I am exhilarated. I wouldn't miss this for the world. Rupan tells us that most people who fall do so while taking photographs: they reach a particularly dramatic view and grab for their camera, and unless their feet are planted firmly on level ground they lose their balance while holding the camera to their eye. Simple as that. And several people have fallen from this place and been killed. It's a sobering thought.

After three hours we reach the plateau and I feel a sense of elation that I have never felt before. We are so high – way above the clouds, with snow-capped mountains all around us. Cheryl and I sit and ponder the meaning of life as we regain control of our breathing. We talk about what it feels like to be fifty and sitting almost on top of the world. I have never understood why people, men in particular, are driven to climb mountains, but now, suddenly, I see what motivates them – the sheer joy of it. The struggle to get there and the overwhelming sense of achievement. The extraordinary view of the world from this pinnacle. The elation that women experience in childbirth and perhaps men only experience when they climb mountains.

We almost run down the track back to camp, doing it in half the time it took us to ascend. Not such a good idea, as we both end up with thumping great headaches and nausea, but even that doesn't dampen our joy at what we have just shared. We eat some lunch with the group then continue our descent, knowing that in just a few days we will be back in Pokhara, in civilisation, with phones, proper toilets, showers and other home comforts.

The first thing I do when we reach Pokhara is find a telephone and contact David. I am concerned that if news of our exciting adventure in the forest has reached Australia he will be beside himself with worry. When I call he's not there, so I leave a message. I call back later and he sounds very upset. No, he hadn't heard about our misadventures. But he has some terrible news. Michael O'Shaughnessy, the 'boy next door' for our children's entire childhood and one of their oldest friends, has died suddenly and without apparent cause while on duty with the Rural Fire Service in Katoomba. And Rick, the young Canadian man so badly injured in the Bali bombings, has also died. They were both in their early thirties. I am plunged, quickly and painfully, right back into the real world.

We have a final dinner in Pokhara and the group presents me with a brilliant orange T-shirt with 'Are the Himalayas Steep?' embroidered across the front. Over a chilled local beer I ask everyone about their personal highlight of the trip. 'The mountains', 'the views' 'the villages' 'the people' are the standard responses but all agree that the highlight was probably getting lost in the forest. They will dine out on it for years, and it's a night that none of us will ever forget.

I am so happy to be going home, and when David meets me in Sydney I am genuinely overjoyed to see him. We are both filled with relief that I am back home for at least six months. It will give us time to sort through all the issues we have confronted over the last year, and time for things between us to settle down a little. We spend the night at an airport hotel because the flight arrived very late; the plan is to drive home at our leisure the next day. Despite feeling exhausted from the long journey we make love and I am amazed at my feeling of desire and passion for him. I can't quite fathom how falling in love with another man and having an affair can be the catalyst for a rekindling of intimacy between husband and wife, but this is what is happening. It's as though we are clinging to each other for dear life after surviving a traumatic ordeal.

On the way home he tells me that a serious drought has set in over the past three months but I am not prepared for the bleak vista that greets me as we drive over the mountains and down to the western plains. The lush green paddocks of last year are burnt brown and white and most of the dams look half-empty. It's a dusty, barren landscape. As we appoach Yetholme, David tells me to be prepared for a shock. 'You won't recognise the farm,' he says. 'It looks terrible.'

As we come up the drive I see that the sweeping lawns have disappeared; and it looks as though they have been soaked in bleach. Only the dandelions seem to have survived. The rest is almost white and crunchy underfoot. What I am not prepared for is that David hasn't watered any of my pot plants. As if the dead lawn and paddocks aren't enough of a shock, the sight of dozens of dead twigs sitting in large terracotta tubs around the back verandah leaves me speechless. We have unlimited house water from a deep spring, and it would have been just a matter of watering them every few days. Even the succulents are dead, and it's almost impossible to kill those.

'What happened here?' I ask, trying not to sound too upset. I don't want us to start off on the wrong foot.

He looks amazed. 'I suppose I didn't even notice them,' he confesses, as if seeing them for the first time. It occurs to me that he'd had a lot of other things on his mind. 'You didn't ask me to water them,' he adds.

Down in the vegetable garden the 400 broad bean plants I put in have also died. I shrug my shoulders. It doesn't really matter; after all, they're only plants. I can grow more when the drought is over.

David takes me proudly out to the poultry yards and introduces me to his babies, the goslings, who by now are almost full grown and very handsome indeed. We take a walk around the farm to survey the situation. The dam is almost dry but the spring and Frying Pan Creek are still flowing. None of the trees looks stressed as yet but the only plant in flower is a carpet rose that I transferred from a pot into the ground just before I left. Roses are remarkably tough, and in most country gardens are among the few plants to survive really prolonged drought.

At another great family reunion I present my seven grandchildren with Nepalese coats and hats that I had had made for them in Pokhara. Little Isabella is still looking very tiny compared with her cousins at the same age, but she is a smiling, gorgeous baby content to lie on the floor on a blanket while the older ones dance and play around her. They lie on top of her and smother her with kisses – I sometimes wonder how she can survive such rough treatment – but she giggles her way through the day, thriving on being the baby of the family.

In November we have some rain, really good rain, and, although the dam doesn't fill, the lawn and paddocks turn green again almost overnight. The lawn actually needs mowing for the first time this year and I feel a burst of energy and enthusiasm for the garden for the first time since we arrived. I weed some of the beds around the house and start to plant the vegetable garden in earnest. It's late spring, which is the perfect time for planting in this climate. I put in three rows of herbs, annual and perennial, four or five different varieties of thyme and sage, oregano, sweet marjoram, basil, coriander, chives, Italian and curly parsley, rocket and various salad greens. I go to town on the tomatoes, planting about forty in neat rows with wooden stakes and trellis for support, plus dwarf beans, borlotti beans, climbing beans, runner beans, silver beet, sweet corn and four very long rows of potatoes, which Miriam's boys help me plant. Within a week everything is sprouting and I mulch furiously between the rows with thick layers of newspaper and straw. I also create a new garden bed along the back verandahs and plant it with drought-tolerant shrubs and perennials – lavender, roses, catmint, ornamental grasses, artemisia and cranesbill geraniums. There's a little more rain, and as the weather gets warmer everything flourishes. The plants seem to double in size every week and I am thankful for such soil and growing conditions. I get a sense that this is part of my healing process, and I come to understand that getting back into the garden helps me feel 'normal' again.

Things between David and me are much calmer and more settled. There has been a major shift in our relationship. Where once we ran around all day being busy and getting on with our lives, allowing few moments for intimacy, we now make a deliberate effort to set aside time for each other. The mornings are spent working, and David also sticks carefully to his exercise regime. But we try to have lunch together in a restaurant at least once or twice a week, and we often spend part of the afternoon in bed, which feels decadent..I don't get as much time for gardening, but what the hell, it's much more fun. In many ways this aspect of our relationship is better now than it has ever been. We have stopped talking about what happened in France earlier in the year. We have said everything that can be said and going over and over it just seems to prolong the pain. We put it aside and move on.

We decide to kill a gosling for our Christmas lunch and, although initially resistant, David finally agrees. But he won't be the one to do the dastardly deed. Rick has volunteered and Miriam is keen to do the plucking. She has never helped with this part of the process before. We rapidly discover that plucking a goose is a lot more work than plucking a rooster. Underneath the thick covering of feathers is a carpet of fine down that is extremely tedious to remove. I want to save the feathers for making pillows, and she painstakingly drops each handful of feathers and down into a pillowslip. It takes hours – no wonder people gave up killing their own poultry and happily started buying chickens from the supermarket instead. There just aren't enough hours in the day for goose plucking. I perform the gruesome gutting process, saving the kidneys and liver for the stuffing, and then singe the entire bird over the gas stove to remove the last of the down. After plucking and dressing it looks small and pathetic, and we all feel rather sorry for it by the time we wrap it up and put it in the fridge.

Two days before Christmas I am alone at the farm when the weather suddenly changes, with dark clouds scooting overhead and a storm brewing. The skies open and rain pours down, within minutes turning into hailstones that pound the corrugated iron roof, becoming louder each minute. I stare out the window, incredulous. It gets heavier and more furious, and the entire landscape turns to white within five minutes, blanketed with a thick covering of icy balls. It stops as quickly as it began and I run outside, almost falling as my feet slip on the icy covering that has smothered the pathways. The hailstones are thirty centimetres deep outside the kitchen door and even deeper on the eastern side of the house. The new garden bed beside the verandah is in tatters. The foliage is shredded, every plant reduced to a fraction of its size. Half the soil and mulch has washed down the path and up against the outside toilet block.

I slither around to the vegetable garden and survey it with horror. There's nothing left. It's all been smashed to the ground in a pulp of shredded leaves. I don't know whether to laugh or cry. The fruit and nut trees have also been brutally damaged.

Very little remains on the trees and what is there is badly bruised and battered.

Why did I bother planting anything? If this is living in the country then, as a gardener, it's just too tough for me. I'll go back to letting the weeds grow and buying our vegetables at the supermarket. A quick call around the neighbourhood reveals that everyone in Yetholme has been badly hit. The commercial fruit growers have been devastated, and this helps give me a sence of perspective. Why should I worry about my few rows of tomatoes when some people have lost their entire income for the season? They also reassure me that events like this are very rare. There's hasn't been a heavy hailstorm like this in twenty years or more. I am slightly reassured. And after Christmas and some extra watering the vegetable garden grows by itself, although I doubt I will have any ripe tomatoes this year. The drought intensifies, there are bushfires all over the state and water everywhere is becoming scarce. It's all part of being Australian, especially for those of us who live away from the big cities. In spite of the hardships, I love it.

On Christmas Eve Aaron and Lorna's dog, still a pup, discovers the bag of goose feathers hidden in the shed, and to him they obviously smell irresistible. He rips and shakes the bag, covering the entire back and side lawns with feathers and goose down. We wake to a 'white' Christmas.

36

 When I was a little girl I always tried to be good. It was part of my way of coping within our deeply troubled family. I believed that if I was really good people would love me – and for most of the time it worked. I knew that my mother loved me – she often told me so. And in his own funny way my father loved me too. He just loved himself more. I recently met up with some old girlfriends from infants and primary school and they confirmed that, for most of the time, I was a 'goodie two-shoes'. My friend Annabet, who is writing a book about her childhood growing up in the boatshed at Balmoral Beach, wrote about her own rebelliousness in kindergarten and talked about our stern infants mistress, Miss O'Connor.

'Mary was her favourite,' Annabet wrote. 'She was a pretty girl with a head of red curls and totally opposite to me in personality. Unlike me, Mary was not drawn to the attention of Miss O'Connor by anything other than her goodness. She was sweet and shy while I was boisterous. I feel certain that Miss O'Conner teamed us together so we would mutually benefit from each other's personality traits.'

The girl next door, Toni, had a slightly different perspective, probably because we played together every day and got on each other's nerves sometimes. She recalled, at our recent reunion dinner, how I would get furious at times, go bright red in the face and kick her. So, underneath my good-girl exterior, there was an angry little girl who could sometimes be very bad. If I did something wrong at home – and it can never have been all that bad, because I don't recall being smacked or severely punished – my mother would ruffle my head of curls and recite the little poem about the girl who was 'very, very good, but when she was bad she was horrid'.

By high school my naughty streak had started to emerge. I was generally doing my best to please my teachers and peers. I was the senior girls prefect, head of the debating team, editor of the school magazine and often the one asked to make speeches on ceremonial occasions such as Anzac Day. But I also started to smoke in the girls' toilets, and to truant at lunchtime and on sports afternoons. I also became politically active and vocal. I helped organise an anti-Vietnam rally of high school students and announced it over the loudspeaker at the Monday school assembly. Prefects were allowed to make announcements without them being vetoed by the staff. This got me into terrible strife – I was stripped of my prefect's badge – and the hypocrisy of it nearly drove me to leave school completely. At the same assembly a spotty youth from the school Christian Fellowship invited fellow students to attend a Billy Graham Crusade at the showground. Why was a religious announcement acceptable but an anti-war message deemed disruptive?

I took my good-girl behaviour into adulthood, always trying to please everyone in the hope that they would love me. I wanted to be a good friend, a good journalist, a good mother, a good wife, a good gardener, always giving the impression that I was happy and that my life was perfect. I still had a wild streak, but I strove to keep it under control. In truth, I wasn't always happy, and when, from time to time, I hit rock bottom, David was the only one to see it. It used to worry him tremendously, because my bad moments were usually manifested in some sort of serious illness that was the result of me pushing myself too hard, striving to achieve and fulfil all the expectations I had for myself. Friends, work colleagues and people in the gardening world would frequently comment, 'I don't know how you do it. Where do you have the time to do all the things that you do? Where do you get the energy?'

It was mental energy, of course, and feeling driven to succeed.

Looking back on the past two years I reflect on what has happened in my life. It's complex and layered, not just a simple matter of going through menopause or feeling a bit bored or disgruntled with a long relationship. It's more about me and how I am feeling about myself than it is about anyone else in my life.

First, I acknowledge the fact that I am dreading the prospect of leaving youth behind. Aging, especially physically, is a process that I cannot accept graciously. While I love being the mother of adult children and I love my seven beautiful grandchildren, I don't like the fact that being 'old' is part of the equation. I still want to dance on the tables and swing from the chandeliers, not potter in my garden with a straw hat and an apron. Like the men who go through a classic mid-life crisis and ditch their faithful wife of twenty-five years and go off with a young blonde, I feel a dread of being too old or too unattractive to appeal sexually to men. It's ridiculous and pathetic, but for me – and I think for many women of my age – it's real and very unsettling. I realise that I am far too anxious about my appearance, which is ironic because for most of my adult life I didn't give two hoots about the way I looked. But now, when I catch a glimpse of myself in a mirror or shop window, I am mortified that the aging process is accelerating and that I am starting to look more and more like my mother when she was an old woman. This is another common fear that women experience – the thought of turning into a carbon copy of their mother. I am shocked by my dismay at the thought. In many ways, I am fighting to turn back the clock, which I realise is impossible, but emotionally find difficult to avoid.

As for the love affair that caused so much pain for David and other members of my family, on one level it truly appals me. But for myself alone I don't have a moment's regret. The sheer power of it, combined with the excitement and mischievous fun of being such a bad girl, was addictive. I know it was selfish, but somehow I just couldn't help myself. The fact that it turned out to be such a rare and lovely experience adds to my determination never to look back at what happened with anguish.

Life will go on. The house in France will have a new kitchen and there will be more walking and trekking tours. I will continue to nurture my precious new relationship with my sister and I will strive to be a saner and more reasonable wife to David. The farm will grow more beautiful and more bountiful and there will probably be more grandchildren to sit around the long table in the dining room. In ten or fifteen years, given our family record for having babies young, I might be a great-grandmother. By then, perhaps I will have come to terms with my life and be content to sit by the fire and grow old.

Also by Mary Moody and available from Murdoch Books

AU REVOIR

Living the good life in the Blue Mountains in New South Wales with her husband, four grown-up children and four (and counting) grandchildren, Mary Moody's life was full. At fifty, she had built a satisfying career as a writer and television presenter which allowed her time for herself, a chance to reflect on life and its meaning. Like many women of her generation, caught up with the commitments of work and family. Mary had never had a moment alone – so she decided to say *au revoir*. She ran away to live on her own for six glorious months in the rural paradise of southwest France.

Au Revoir is the story of Mary's solo journey. It is funny, warm and reflective, as Mary adapts to life as a single person in the Lot, one of the most remote and beautiful parts of France. Revelling in the food, seasons and characters she encountered, Mary gained new insight into herself while enjoying life to the full. Her account of an escape – with its exhilarating freedom, new experiences and chance for renewal – will inspire every reader to run away from home.